S0-BDN-476

LOOKING OUT FOR #2

BY BRUCE MILES

Copyright @ 2010 by Bruce Miles

All rights reserved. With the exception of the appendix, no parts of this publication may be reproduced or transmitted in any form or by any means, electronic or mechanical, including photocopy, recording, or any information storage and retrieval system, without permission in writing from the publisher.

Appendix items can be copied for personal use.

For sections other than the appendix, requests for permission to make copies of parts of the work should be submitted online at *www.bigrivergroup.com*.

www.bigrivergroup.com

ISBN-10: 1-934478-24-5
ISBN-13: 978-1-934478-24-0

Designed by Paul Wilson

Printed in the United States of America

TABLE OF CONTENTS

CHAPTER 1

CREATING
FOLLOWERSHIP

"Healthy followership is a real, genuine employee response to healthy, genuine leadership, especially if that leadership is clear about the vision for the organization, and a good plan is in place to achieve that vision."

Over the past two decades, I have had the privilege to assist organizations throughout the United States and Canada in the areas of better strategic planning ("Chainsaw Planning"©), more effective hiring and evaluation techniques, managing conflict and difficult employees, and leadership and "followership" training.

The topic of followership has long fascinated me. I have found that followership is an essential element within my most effective clients' organizations. Healthy followership is a real, genuine employee response to healthy, genuine leadership, especially if that leadership is clear about the vision for the organization, and a good plan is in place to achieve that vision.

Effective Organizations

At one point, I was thinking about my most effective clients and discovered that a key differentiator for those organizations was the presence of a strong, effective No. 2 person. The No. 2 is the backbone of the business: The person owners rely on when they cannot or do not have the personal resources to attend to business on their own. Business owners trust and expect their No. 2s to manage their business as if it were their own. These are the people who can:

- Think like an owner;
- Model effective, healthy followership;
- Understand, promote and help deliver the organizational vision;

- Manage outcomes identified as essential within the strategic plan;
- Help employees to persist, succeed, and thrive;
- Learn new skills; and
- Deal with some role ambiguity (because we don't have it all figured out).

A Decision-Making Tool

In this book, you will learn ways to accurately select your No. 2 person and how to delegate essential duties. You will read stories from owners who have brought No. 2s along effectively and also benefit from some examples of what not to do.

To assemble this book, I have spent hours hunkered down interviewing No. 2s in businesses of varying size, sector and style. They each bring their own perspective, but the commonalities are staggering. Just as it takes a particular personality and intellect to own or sit at the top of a company's hierarchy, it takes a particular individual to chase the carrot, meet the organization's goals and not get hung up on who gets the glory.

"No. 2s have shared with me what makes them happy, and more importantly, what makes them stay."

No. 2s have shared with me what makes them happy, and, more importantly, what makes them stay. Some of the 2's in this book started out in the No. 2 position and some naturally transitioned due to their drive and personality.

Resources Made Easy

No. 2s are in always in high demand. The economy does not affect their ability to be wooed away by another company. Good leaders know the importance of their second-in-command and they understand (or should understand) what it takes to make them productive, and ultimately, happy. I'm not talking money here – job satisfaction takes on numerous dimensions and salary is just one piece of the puzzle.

Many examples, forms, and worksheets are noted in the book and listed in the appendix. Each of those resources are also available for free on the Big River Group website: *bigrivergroup.com*. I hope they are of help to you as you select and make progress with your No. 2.

I've also included a list of questions at the end of each chapter to guide your journey and help you accomplish some key elements in each chapter. If you can say yes to each of the questions, then you are ready to move to the next chapter – and the next step in this process of creating a highly effective organization. This book is intended to be an engaging process, not a passive end-of-the-day read. I will give you tools and make resources easily accessible so you can dig in and, by the end of this book, have a clear set of plans to bring in a solid No. 2.

If at any point in this book, you would like to contact me for more detail, clarification, or to let me know that you have a serious disconnect with the ideas, please feel free to contact me at *bruce@bigrivergroup.com*. I will be happy to visit with you and help you get as much out of the book as possible.

Now, let's get started finding your No. 2.

CHAPTER 2

STRATEGY BEFORE
THE SEARCH

*"Past behavior is the best predictor of
future behavior."*

Prior to my first day of kindergarten, my dear old dad
gave me a lesson in followership. He kept it simple and
said, "If your teacher says jump, you ask, 'How high
and how often?'" I was only five, but I thought, 'I get it.'
I pride myself on being a good follower and like many
leaders in the business world, it has served me well. The
trouble is that not all of our workers think that way.

In every organization, there are three types of people: the overachiever, the backbone, and the butthead. Here is how they spread out in any organization:

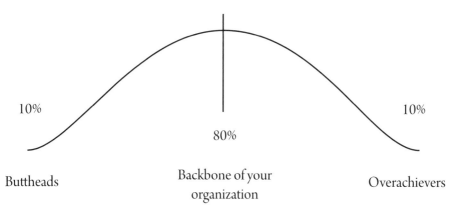

10%   80%   10%

Buttheads   Backbone of your   Overachievers
                    organization

It's that 10 percent of overachievers on the right side of the bell curve that really drives an organization. They stand out from day one. They ask how high they should jump and they regularly jump without being asked. They come early and they stay late. These workers think like an owner. They anticipate issues and suggest solutions. It's in that 10 percent of overachievers that every successful No. 2 has been found. The reason is simple. Past behavior is the best predictor of future behavior.

It's that common truth that often leads organizations to spend extensive resources – time and money – trying to recruit a No. 2 from another organization. Owners want that sought-after candidate, and may rush to promote one, or hire too optimistically without enough due diligence.

Many times, the best place for owners to find candidates for their No. 2 spot is inside the organization. These potential candidates already understand the company's systems, goals, products and services. They have specific and essential knowledge of where the company is going and why.

Often, it is easy for No. 1s to see the big picture and even look into the future, but they can get bogged down in the details of how to get started on finding a No. 2. So, here are three steps No. 1s can take to get started today:

Step 1: Take a short break to specify your vision

Before deciding who will hold the No. 2 spot, it's critical that owners articulate their five-year vision. Here is mine: A 43-foot sail boat in the southern tropics with my feet up and an adult beverage. You may laugh, but no one has ever told me that they don't understand it. What's most important about this vision is that it is clear.

I do not leave much room for interpretation and that's how clear a vision should be.

Although that is the vision in my head, in all seriousness, I also have a more traditional vision. Here is Big River's ideal destination:

> *"To touch and help even greater numbers of leaders and teams in business, education, nonprofits and government across the Midwest, United States and throughout the world. To help those leaders and teams through direct service, web-based resources, ITV and teleconferences."*

A Visioning Worksheet (Appendix 1) can help owners transfer their vision to paper and effectively communicate it. Fred Bursch had decades of experience leading and operating Bursch Travel (*burschtravel.com*) before bringing in a No. 2 to manage the daily operations and further position the Midwestern travel agency for growth. He knew what needed to get done and he did it all until that point.

But when Lee Hurd started to assume higher-priority No. 2 responsibilities, Fred will admit that transferring that vision to her did not happen effectively. At the same time, Bursch Travel faced the unforeseen devastating effect 9/11 had on the travel industry. A lack of clarity left Lee wondering if she was leading the organization in the right direction. That changed after Fred outlined his vision. Within a couple of hours, Fred used the visioning worksheet to clearly specify his expectations for the agency's growth, productivity, profitability and corporate sales as well as accountability and his daily involvement in the future.

The exercise allowed Fred to think more deeply about each of those elements and better communicate them to Lee. By seeing it on paper, Lee understood the vision and found that she could work harder and faster to achieve the company's vision. Lee immediately assembled all senior management and helped them set departmental goals, all aligned with the vision.

Taking regular timeouts with employees to share the vision also can serve as an effective testing ground for finding a No. 2. Start talking more about where the business is headed and what it will take to achieve the goals. The better employees will start to ask questions and adjust their efforts to help make it happen. The message will start to trickle down and help other employees stay focused, too.

Step 2: Identify specific skills needed for your No. 2

Before action-oriented owners start zeroing in on the perfect No. 2, they need to take a look at their own talents and skills. What are the most valuable skills they bring to the organization? No, it's not always easy. No. 1s need to be brutally honest with themselves and not be afraid of the raw answer. Determining what owners want – and need – in a No. 2 starts with evaluating their own strengths and weaknesses. That helps owners shape the skill sets and experience levels that the organization will need from a No. 2 to be more effective. An owner may realize that he or she excels in finance and operations, so perhaps the No. 2 should bring more sales skills to the organization.

Tara Tollefson, owner of The Buzz Company (*buzz-company.com*), a small research-based customer relations and marketing firm, reached a point in the business' growth when she needed an assistant to come inside and help her stay on track as her list of clients and opportunities grew. Strong organization and communication skills were a must. The person also needed to bring solid office support skills to the business.

Focused on her vision of growing the business and expanding its services, Tara also looked for a golden

"Before action-oriented owners start zeroing in on the perfect No. 2, they need to take a look at their own talents and skills."

nugget in her No. 2. She found it in Pam Nelson, who had spent much of her life and career working as a professional speaker and performer with religious organizations. Pam's golden nugget was her ability to create captivating videos and unveil the richness of a story.

Soon after bringing Pam on board, Tara added Buzzmaker videos to the list of the company's signature services. In a short time, the videos proved to be a strong revenue source and in less than a year, they had helped to elevate the company's image to another level. Tara's vision for the company was essential to her search and resulted in an exceptional hire and an exceptional No. 2.

Step 3: Hard skills are great, but don't forget the soft skills

Another cornerstone of the identification process is not only outlining the hard skills, but also the equally important soft skills the No. 2 needs to possess for future success. The Hard Skills, Soft Skills worksheet (at the end of this chapter and Appendix 3) is designed to help owners specify what skills are needed as they search for their No. 2.

And remember those buttheads! It's important to find a No. 2 with the skills to effectively work with those people and their issues. Some people can really shine when put in this situation. I've seen it firsthand time and again. During a company-wide visioning session, I stood in the back of the conference room listening to a leader share some strategic points and motivate the employees to better performance. Not long into the presentation, one worker shared his complete discontentment. His brash approach threatened to erode the leader's message.

The tension in the room reached a high level as everyone else wondered how the leader would respond. The leader walked closer to the worker as the tantrum escalated. He walked behind the employee, put his hands on the worker's shoulders, and began to speak – calmly. The worker simmered down and the leader demonstrated his ability to handle even the toughest rivals.

That may not be the way that most of us deal with a butthead, but clearly identifying the hard and soft skills for a No. 2 will help to ensure that owners not only select the right candidate, but also that they set that person up for ongoing success with the majority of employees in the organization. The skills charts below helps owners begin to map their path to finding a No. 2.

YOUR ROUTE TO WAAAAAY BETTER HIRING

DESIRED HARD SKILLS	DESIRED SOFT SKILLS
Clearly define at least 5 Hard Skills. Hard skills comprise the technical requirements of the job. These skills fall into the following areas: • Technical expertise • Experience in specific software of system technologies • Hardware	Clearly define at least 5 Soft Skills. Soft skills include personality traits, social graces and personal habits, and should complement the hard skills listed in the first column. These skills fall into the following areas: • Emotional intelligence • Interpersonal skills • Behavioral traits

In the chart below, see how these hard and soft skills could play out when an organization is looking to hire a sales manager, one of the most desired No. 2 positions.

SALES MANAGER

DESIRED HARD SKILLS	DESIRED SOFT SKILLS
• Experience with multiple client management systems. • Experience holding staff accountable for upstream activity. • Ability to set sales goals for company, product, department, and individual salespersons. • Frequent experience in meeting and exceeding goals. • Ability to train on cold calling. • Knowledge of relationship-based sales. • Efficiency in database and word processing software.	• Ability to follow owner's lead. • Ability to finesse owner on decision making. • Experience supervising a variety of sales personalities. • Experience differentiating sales instruction to match employees' personalities and motivations • Tendency to be hard on the problem, easy on the people. • High level of emotional intelligence. • Solid planning and time management skills.

Owners can use the Skills Worksheet (on page 17 or Appendix 3) to identify the hard and soft skills they need in a No. 2.

No. 2 Position Title: _____

Desired Hard Skills	Desired Soft Skills
1.	1.
2.	2.
3.	3.
4.	4.
5.	5.

"Begin with the end in mind."

Begin with the end in mind. Taking the time on the front end is critical to selection success. To use a carpenter's motto, it is better to measure twice and cut once. Owners can consider their vision and lists of hard and soft skills as their measurements. Those items will help the organization develop clear expectations, responsibilities and a growth plan for the future No. 2.

Are you ready?

If you can answer yes to these three questions, you're ready to move forward:

✓ Have I clearly identified my vision for the organization?

✓ Do I really know what skill sets are needed for my No. 2?

✓ Have I determined if I can give this position to someone inside the organization?

Toolbox

Use these tools to get started today. Visit *bigrivergroup.com* or flip to the Appendix for an electronic or printer-friendly versions. Gray indicates tools not yet discussed. Bold indicates tools introduced in this chapter:

Visioning Worksheet
Helps owners transfer their vision to paper and effectively communicate it. (Appendix 1)

Sample Visions
A look at how other No. 1s have put the Visioning Worksheet into practice. (Appendix 2)

Hard Skills'/Soft Skills' Worksheet
Helps owners specify what skills are needed as they search for their No. 2. (Appendix 3)

Resume Review Worksheet
Provides method to identify top candidates for No. 2 job. (Appendix 4)

Email Response Worksheet
Helps evaluate the responses to each emailed question on a three-point scale. (Appendix 5)

Interview Score Sheet
Provides scoring scale to evaluate in-depth questions based on emailed responses. (Appendix 6)

Priorities Worksheet
An owner's guide to articulating a new, perfect destination for their organizations. (Appendix 7)

Priorities to Goals Worksheet
Similar to the Priorities Worksheet, an owner's guide to translating a vision into priorities and goals. (Appendix 8)

Planning Funnel
Provides a planning process to stay on task, increase buy-in and develop a strategic plan that won't gather dust. (Appendix 9)

Outcome Diagnosis Worksheet
A planning tool that helps individuals or a team of individuals identify intended and unintended successes and challenges. (Appendix 10)

Goal Work Plan
A tool to engage a team of employees in creating a well-defined plan of action in less than 30 minutes. (Appendix 11)

My Job, Your Job
Helps translate the owners' vision into priorities and desired outcomes. (Appendix 12)

Employee Feedback Tool
Reinforces the progress of a No. 2 and provides clear, consistent expectations on their roles. (Appendix 13)

Chapter 3

Selecting the Best

"Most traditional hiring approaches are flawed and unreliable."

Many business owners make the same overly-optimistic mistake when hiring a No. 2. They review resumes and parade a series of candidates through interviews and then "go with their gut." This is flawed for more than one reason, but here is the key problem. Candidates may lie, or overstate their capabilities, on resumes and they can be less than truthful in the interviews. The net result is that either the owner spends too much valuable owner-time training the person and explaining what they need, or the owner eventually searches again for another No. 2.

Most traditional hiring approaches are flawed and unreliable. Harry Brull, senior vice president of public sector services for Personnel Decisions International (*personneldecisions.com*), thinks resumes and interviews are typically the least reliable tools for hiring talented employees.

Landing the best candidate requires a strategic, systematic approach. But it should not demand all of the owner's time. It's not OK to interview nine people for a job. No one can effectively track nine candidates. Leaders need to narrow the pool to 3-4 candidates for better interviews. Is that possible? Well, it requires leaders to reverse their thinking about the interview process.

Step 1: Sort and score

Start by reviewing the submitted resumes and supporting materials from a pool of candidates and narrow it down to a dozen candidates or less using the lists of hard and soft skills needed and the five-year vision for the organization. Use the Resume Review Score Sheet (Appendix 4) to identify the top candidates.

Then, make those candidates *earn* an interview.

Step 2: Conduct an e-mail interview

The traditional face-to-face interview tests an individual's ability to make decisions quickly, but, in truth, most jobs do not require that. The No. 2 spot often calls the individual to think strategically, see the big picture and take a more systematic approach to position the company for future success.

Through e-mail, owners can give the candidates the opportunity to flex their strategic muscles and really communicate their abilities. Using key objectives the organization would like to achieve over the next several years, No. 1s can craft a series of direct questions that will ask the candidates to describe their experience in each specific area.

Crafting Effective E-mail Interviews

- Identify at least five key issues facing your organization in the five years. Turn those issues into the questions.
- Start each question with "Tell me about a specific time when you had to..." or "Explain your experience with..."
- At the end of each question, ask for a reference who can speak to that specific experience for the applicant.
- Limit e-mailed interview to 6-8 questions.

E-mail the candidates and ask them what 24-hour period in the next seven days they would like complete an e-mail interview. Send the questions at their requested time and soon you will find who is experienced in the areas you need and who has the knowledge necessary to handle the job.

Bill Worzala, a candidate for a clinic administration position within St. Cloud Orthopedics, was floored when he first received the list of questions asking him to explain his experience in specific areas and then identify references that could corroborate his answers.

Sample E-mailed Questions

- Tell us about a time when you had to correct a doctor who was underperforming.
- Out of all the medical information management systems, which do you prefer and why?
- Explain your experience setting up or growing satellite offices for a medical clinic.

The questions were explicit: Tell us about a time when you had to correct a doctor who was underperforming. Out of all the medical information management systems, which do you prefer and why? Explain your experience setting up or growing satellite offices for a medical clinic. Each question called him to go beyond the typically shallow resume and explain his successes.

His heart was pumping. He knew it was do or die. Forget the firm handshake, eye contact and first words he may say when he first enters the traditional face-to-face interview. He knew his first impression would be in that e-mail. How could he make himself stand out? How could he tactfully answer questions about experience that he knew he did not have?

With time ticking, he read every question, resisting the temptation to provide an immediate answer. When he lacked experience in an area, he explained what he would do in that situation. He wanted to show that he was a big picture thinker and was not afraid of a challenge.

Not knowing it, Bill had just made a slam dunk. The e-mail interview does favor the experienced, but does not necessarily undervalue the less experienced.

"It evaluates each candidate's ability to work within a deadline, follow directions, employ organization strategies and communicate."

It evaluates each candidate's ability to work within a deadline, follow directions, employ organization strategies and communicate. It always amazes me how candidates respond. Some return the questions carefully formatted and spell checked. One applicant stated that he would not participate in this process, but looked forward to scheduling an interview in which he could explain his experiences. Are you kidding me? That response spoke volumes about his style, and his resume landed in the "Thanks, we will keep your resume on file" pile.

Step 3: Score the e-mailed responses

Scoring the e-mailed responses provides a good opportunity to engage some key employees in the process. These employees can use the E-mail Response Worksheet (Appendix 5) to evaluate the responses to each of the questions on a 3-point scale with +, 0, or -. Owners should give employees the freedom to add a little extra credit to a candidate's score and provide reasoning as appropriate. Then owners can tally the columns for a final score and narrow the pool to 3-4 top candidates to bring in for interviews.

But before they do, it's important that leaders call their references to determine if each of their answers is true or exaggerated. The time owners spend here also will allow owners to arm themselves with additional insight and detailed information for the interview. It is time well spent. Skipping this step can hurt the entire process and future success of a No. 2.

Step 4: Conduct a face-to-face interview

When it comes time for the face-to-face interviews, owners cannot revert back to the dozens of surface questions traditionally asked during a conventional interview. Really, what does an answer to a question like "If you were a book in the library, what would you be and why?" really tell you. This is a No. 2 you're looking for. Dig in deeper.

Owners should allow the e-mailed questions to create some of the content for the face-to-face interviews and rely on the Interview Score Sheet (see Appendix 6) to guide their final decision. Start by choosing 4-5 questions from the e-mailed list to ask about in more detail during the hour interview. This gives candidates a second chance to respond, but also allows owners to challenge them to get more specific information regarding implementation in the owner's company.

It's important for the questions to be relevant. If the vision has changed slightly since the e-mailed interviews, then owners need to craft new questions and let the candidates know beforehand about the change. Then, when candidates arrive for the interviews, give them the new material on paper and let them have an hour to think about the new collection of questions and be prepared to respond during the interview.

While the process stretched Bill's thinking, he admits that the e-mailed interview better prepared him for his face-to-face interview. It gave him time to thoughtfully consider what he would bring to the position and the organization. He was able to spend 30 minutes on his answer to each question – instead of 30 seconds.

After the face-to-face interviews were complete, the medical group owners knew exactly what they were getting and could easily identify who best would serve the organization through its strategic growth cycle outlined in the five-year plan.

Today, Bill still pulls out the e-mail he sent to the medical group and reads his responses. They provide a path to handling the issues the clinic is now facing.

The result has bottom line benefits. The medical group has been able to successfully execute its expansion plan, opening multiple satellite offices in three years and substantially growing its network.

Are you ready?

If you can answer yes to these three questions, you're ready to move forward:

✓ Have I designed a system that's so tight that people can't get an interview out of me without proving their worth in advance?

✓ Have I built a way for my key employees to have some input on answers to emails and face-to-face interviews?

✓ Do I have enough information from semi-finalists to select a No. 2?

Toolbox

Use these tools to get started today. Visit *bigrivergroup.com* or flip to the Appendix for an electronic or printer-friendly versions. Gray indicates tools not yet discussed. Bold indicates tools introduced in this chapter:

Visioning Worksheet
Helps owners transfer their vision to paper and effectively communicate it. (Appendix 1)

Sample Visions
A look at how other No. 1s have put the Visioning Worksheet into practice. (Appendix 2)

Hard Skills'/Soft Skills' Worksheet
Helps owners specify what skills are needed as they search for their No. 2. (Appendix 3)

Resume Review Worksheet
Provides method to identify top candidates for No. 2 job. (Appendix 4)

Email Response Worksheet
Helps evaluate the responses to each emailed question on a three-point scale. (Appendix 5)

Interview Score Sheet
Provides scoring scale to evaluate in-depth questions based on emailed responses. (Appendix 6)

Priorities Worksheet
An owner's guide to articulating a new, perfect destination for their organizations. (Appendix 7)

Priorities to Goals Worksheet
Similar to the Priorities Worksheet, an owner's guide to translating a vision into priorities and goals. (Appendix 8)

Planning Funnel
Provides a planning process to stay on task, increase buy-in and develop a strategic plan that won't gather dust. (Appendix 9)

Outcome Diagnosis Worksheet
A planning tool that helps individuals or a team of individuals identify intended and unintended successes and challenges. (Appendix 10)

Goal Work Plan
A tool to engage a team of employees in creating a well-defined plan of action in less than 30 minutes. (Appendix 11)

My Job, Your Job
Helps translate the owners' vision into priorities and desired outcomes. (Appendix 12)

Employee Feedback Tool
Reinforces the progress of a No. 2 and provides clear, consistent expectations on their roles. (Appendix 13)

Chapter 4

Sharing the Plan

"Once I finally saw it on paper, I could work harder and faster because I knew where we were going."

- Lee Hurd, No. 2 at Bursh Travel

When the owner of a leading travel agency bought another branch and merged two locations, he saw a spark in a young sales' person. With great sales' performance and complementary personality, Fred Bursch identified her as a perfect No. 2. Not long after the acquisition, she became his No. 2 and has eventually become the vice president of operations.

But, as I began to share in Chapter 2, over time, and specifically after 9/11, the duo struggled to meet the owner's goals. As the No. 2, Lee generally understood where the owner wanted to go, however, with minimal documentation that clarified the owner's vision, she became frustrated. She wanted to move the business forward, but the specific destination was not clear. At one critical point, the business and the relationship between No. 1 and No. 2 had just about reached the breaking point.

Lee was close to walking away when the duo sat down to evaluate the organization, their relationship and a future plan. Fred and Lee agree that one of the most organization-changing products of that meeting was the eventual development of Fred's five-year vision for the agency. For Lee, the vision provided the final destination, and the plan provided the navigational beacons. "Once I finally saw it on paper, I could work harder and faster because I knew where we were going," Lee said.

Sharing No. 1's Vision

Small and medium business owners rarely take the time to describe their vision (the perfect destination) to their No. 2. Instead, owners typically talk about urgent matters such as deadlines, personnel issues, schedules, supply and vendor issues, etc. But the regular review of the vision is among the most essential tasks for orienting a No. 2 for ongoing success.

This clear vision for the company extends beyond a mission statement and beyond philosophical principles or core values for the company. The vision statement needs to specifically describe the owner's mental picture for the company and should look out at least 3-5 years. The vision should be supported by hard data as well as soft data. The hard data is based on balance sheets, profit and loss statements, sales' projections and other reports. The soft data includes the perceptions of the company's customers, employees, vendors and other interested parties.

"It's not enough for an owner to have that clear vision in mind. Putting it on paper is essential."

It's not enough for an owner to have that clear vision in mind – putting it on paper is essential. It is not only an effective way to communicate it to No. 2 and other employees, but it also proves to be a productive exercise for the owner. Dr. Jeff Nelson, a veterinarian and owner of Granite City Pet Hospital (*granitecitypet.com*), knew where he wanted to take his practice. He tried to relay it verbally to his staff, but he failed to effectively make the vision clear and compelling enough for employees.

He's not alone. Many owners struggle to clearly communicate their vision to their employees and the organization suffers because of it. The Vision Worksheet, referenced in Chapter 2 (Appendix 1), becomes even more critical once No. 1s have selected a No. 2. If the vision has not been clearly outlined at this point, No. 1s now need to take the time to set priorities and communicate them on paper. The Vision Worksheet, Priorities Worksheet (Appendix 7) or Priorities to Goals Worksheet (Appendix 8) serve as an owner's guide to articulating a new, perfect destination for their organizations.

"Many owners struggle to clearly communicate their vision to their employees and the organization suffers because of it."

Jeff spent about one month thinking about the pet hospital's future in key areas. He used the guiding questions on the Vision Worksheet to write clear and concise statements, explaining his goals related to patient care, customer experience, marketing, revenue, staff development and management structure. Using the Priorities to Goals Worksheet, Jeff translated those priorities into key goals:

1. **Priority:** Patient Care
   Goal: To be THE pet hospital in Central Minnesota that people recognize and want to be a part of.

2. **Priority:** Customer Experience
   Goal: To have clients feel like they are welcome and a part of a family.

3. **Priority:** Marketing
   Goal: To reach and educate the greatest number of existing and potential clients.

4. **Priority:** Revenue
   Goal: To increase revenue goals – 8 to 10 percent over the previous year.

5. **Priority:** Staff Development
   Goal: To have a comfortable and informed staff.

6. **Priority:** Management Structure
   Goal: To have a goal-oriented, efficient staff whose focus will allow us to exceed expectations.

The process of completing the Vision Worksheet or Priorities to Goals Worksheet helps owners get specific about important variables such as future sales and revenue mix, marketing efforts, operations, finances, vendors, suppliers' role in the organization, etc. For many No. 1s, this is the first time they have taken the time to think about their vision and leveraging that vision to a greater degree in the company.

Charting the vision and an effective course for the company does not require days of valuable work and owners do not need to do it alone. Once the Vision Worksheet is complete, owners can make it happen in as few as four hours by using the Chainsaw Planning© System and these steps in the Planning Funnel (below or Appendix 9). These tools help No. 2s stay on task, increase buy-in and develop a plan that won't gather dust. Let's review those steps.

Planning Funnel: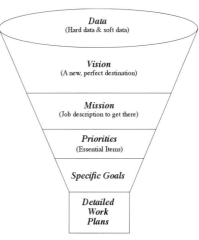

Data
(Hard data & soft data)

Vision
(A new, perfect destination)

Mission
(Job description to get there)

Priorities
(Essential Items)

Specific Goals

Detailed
Work
Plans

Step 1: Dig into the data

Gaining the necessary data and launching the planning process starts with inviting a cross-section of employees, supervisors, management, staff and key outsiders (your accountant, lawyer, mentor, etc.) to a 90-minute session. During this session, commonly held over breakfast or dinner, participants complete steps one through three. The owner starts by presenting the hard data and provides two or three data "snapshots" of the organization over the past 10 or 20 years to create a baseline understanding prior to planning.

Start the meeting by create random small groups; I pass out playing cards to break the participants up by suit. Small groups are more effective because there are no side conversations, everyone speaks more often and participant satisfaction with the process increases.

To gather soft data in this first step, each small group identifies the following items over the last five years in each of the four squares on the Outcome Diagnosis Worksheet (on page 38 or Appendix 10):

- Intended work that yielded successes
- Intended work that turned out less-than positive
- Unanticipated items that yielded great results

- Items that were unanticipated and were tough to handle

Outcome Diagnosis Worksheet:

	Positive	Less Than Positive
Intended	1. 2. 3. 4. 5.	1. 2. 3. 4. 5.
Unintended	1. 2. 3. 4. 5.	1. 2. 3. 4. 5.

Enlarge the Outcome Worksheet and post it on the wall or draw the four boxes on a large flip chart to compile the results of each of the small groups. Through a brief dialogue as a large group, participants will paint a complete picture of the organization.

Step 2: Identify the long-term destination – Vision

For the next step in the Chainsaw Planning© System, No. 1s should have participants break into new small groups and ask each group to identify a company vision – a long-term, perfect destination for the organization five years down the road. Each group then shares the vision and all participants vote to select the best vision.

Starting a Vision Statement

Vision statements describe new destinations.

Ideal organizations:
- "We will become a top-ten university."
- "The best restaurant in town: Your first choice for fine dining."

Ideal services:
- "The auto glass company that provides the best customer service."
- "The family restaurant that provides unmatched attention and service."

Ideal products:
- "Producing flawless vehicles at a reasonable cost."
- "A 200-pound buck hanging in a tree by 10 a.m. on Saturday."

To streamline the voting process, give each participant three sticky dots (or other small sticker) and ask them to place their stickers on the three vision statements they view as most important.

The Vision Worksheet can help accelerate this process. For the travel agency's planning session, Fred outlined his vision for key categories: growth, productivity, accountability, corporate sales, group travel and his daily involvement. For each category, he posed a series of questions for key employees to discuss and answer. Under agency profitability, for an example, he identified his desire to find alternatives to drive revenue during traditionally slow periods. Then, he asked employees to discuss the agency's primary focus and activities during that time, compensation models for agents, and managerial duties.

"Effective mission statements serve as an organization's job description that explains what needs to be done to achieve the vision."

Step 3: Identifying the road to the vision – Mission

Mission statements should not be simply a series of fluffy words that make an organization, its employees or its customers feel good about an ideal purpose. Effective mission statements serve as an organization's job description that explains what needs to be done to achieve the vision.

A clear results-driven mission statement contains four elements:

1. What an organization will do.

2. What services it will provide.

3. What products will be delivered.

4. How lives will be changed.

Mission Statements = Job Descriptions

Here are some examples of each of teh four key elements:

1. What an organization will do.
   - "Provide an excellent university education at an average price."
   - "Provide the best food and the best service in our area."

2. What services will be provided.
   - "We make our customers' lives easier by replacing all auto glass with no disruption in their work or home schedules."
   - "Need credit? Bad credit? We arrange loans for anyone."

3. What products will be delivered.
   - "On-time delivery, every time."
   - "A deer hunt with flawless planning & attention to detail."

4. How lives will be changed.
   - "Providing an exceptional environment with first-class instruction and equipment to help our customers improve fitness."

No. 1s should start by giving some examples of mission statements to help participants focus their thoughts, understand the expectations and begin to spur some ideas.

Then, No. 1s can use the same small group planning process used for the vision to break into small groups and write a mission statement. Each small group then shares the mission statement and all the participants receive three dots to vote on the best mission.

Step 4: Set priorities

In this step, owners use the new vision and mission to identify no more than five or six front-burner priorities to pursue over the next 12 months. These priorities should put the company on the most accurate course for that new destination (vision). Some examples could include:

- *Bring in five new accounts each month for the next four months.*

- *Improve employee training on a specific topic over the next three months.*

- *Expand 12 corporate accounts in the next four months to improve current relationships or solicit additional business.*

The group again will receive three dots to vote on which priorities they view as most pressing. Based on which statements are speckled with the most dots, narrow the priorities to the top four.

Step 5: Set specific goals

No. 1s now can use these new priorities to start a conversation with their No. 2s and encourage them to brainstorm one or two new goals ("the best way to proceed"), aligned with each of the new priorities.

The success of this process relies on engaging No. 2s to think like owners. This exercise is sort of like a coloring book: It provides the outlines of what No. 1s want to work on (new priorities) and asks No. 2s to start to color it in while staying within the lines.

Both Fred and Jeff revisit their goals and priorities regularly. Jeff carries the company's vision to monthly staff meetings where employees discuss and assess various portions of delivery and progress. This allows the veterinary practice to measure progress, stay on track, and involve employees in the process on a regular basis.

At the travel agency, employees not only review the goals each year at the company's annual meeting but also during their own performance reviews throughout the year. Aiming to keep the goals at the forefront of the organization and each employee's job, Lee has developed a feedback system that starts with employees setting personal goals connected to the agency's vision and priorities.

Step 6: Track results

A clear and detailed vision minimizes gray areas, improves overall operations and allows organizations to achieve key results. Without a clear vision, No. 2s – and all staff – lack direction and growth is stifled. At Bursch Travel, Lee admitted to being able to increase her productivity and the organization's overall effectiveness after understanding Fred's five-year vision.

For Fred, the vision planning model gave him a tighter grip on his company's future and allowed him to measure progress. That boosted the chain's bottom line and annual achievements. "I wish we would have done it ten years ago," he said. "We would be much farther ahead now."

Organizations can take this planning process one step farther by creating detailed work plans for each

---

Creating Work Plans

Here's how organizations can translate their priorities and goals into work plans that foster desirable outcomes. For each priority, use the Goal Work Plan Worksheet to identify the following:

1. Admiration of the Problem
   - Identify all sub-issues and hurdles associated with the priority.
   - Complete in 5 minutes.
2. New Goal
   - Articulate in 20 words or less.
   - Complete in 5 minutes.
3. Objectives/Action Steps
   - Identify no more than four specific steps the organization needs to take to achieve the goal.
   - Complete in 10 minutes.
4. Timeline, Resources, Responsibility
   - For each of the objectives, identify a timeline, resources needed and the name of the person responsible for completing it.
   - Complete in 5 minutes.
5. Evaluation Plan
   - Identify quantitative and qualitative benchmarks that the organization will use to measure success of the goal.
   - Complete in 5 minutes.

---

goal. With the help of the Chainsaw Planning© Goal Work Plan (Appendix 11), No. 2s or the diverse planning groups engaged to create the vision and mission can create a well-defined plan of action in less than 30 minutes.

The Work Plan first instructs organizations to define the goal and up to four action steps to achieve it. For each of those four steps, organizations then need to identify a timeline, any resources needed and the person responsible for completing it. The accountability goes even farther by challenging the organization to develop quantitative and qualitative indicators of success.

Are you ready?

If you can answer yes to these four questions, you're ready to move forward:

✓ Do I have a clear vision with enough specifics to guide my No. 2?

✓ Does my No. 2 really understand where we're going in the next 3-5 years, and why we have chosen this destination?

✓ Does my No. 2 have a firm grasp of our priorities and goals for the next 1-2 quarters?

✓ Is my No. 2 asking the right kind of questions to get the job done?

Toolbox

Use these tools to get started today. Visit *bigrivergroup.com* or flip to the Appendix for an electronic or printer-friendly versions. Gray indicates tools not yet discussed. Bold indicates tools introduced in this chapter:

Visioning Worksheet
Helps owners transfer their vision to paper and effectively communicate it. (Appendix 1)

Sample Visions
A look at how other No. 1s have put the Visioning Worksheet into practice. (Appendix 2)

Hard Skills'/Soft Skills' Worksheet
Helps owners specify what skills are needed as they search for their No. 2. (Appendix 3)

Resume Review Worksheet
Provides method to identify top candidates for No. 2 job. (Appendix 4)

Email Response Worksheet
Helps evaluate the responses to each emailed question on a three-point scale. (Appendix 5)

Interview Score Sheet
Provides scoring scale to evaluate in-depth questions based on emailed responses. (Appendix 6)

Priorities Worksheet
An owner's guide to articulating a new, perfect destination for their organizations. (Appendix 7)

Priorities to Goals Worksheet
Similar to the Priorities Worksheet, an owner's guide to translating a vision into priorities and goals. (Appendix 8)

Planning Funnel
Provides a planning process to stay on task, increase buy-in and develop a strategic plan that won't gather dust. (Appendix 9)

Outcome Diagnosis Worksheet
A planning tool that helps individuals or a team of individuals identify intended and unintended successes and challenges. (Appendix 10)

Goal Work Plan
A tool to engage a team of employees in creating a well-defined plan of action in less than 30 minutes. (Appendix 11)

My Job, Your Job
Helps translate the owners' vision into priorities and desired outcomes. (Appendix 12)

Employee Feedback Tool
Reinforces the progress of a No. 2 and provides clear, consistent expectations on their roles. (Appendix 13)

Chapter 5

Intentional Leadership

Everyone is different. That's a lesson I learned in school when I was just a pip-squeak. But as a business leader in today's evolving working world and as a consultant to many businesses facing the new realities, I am constantly reminded of this age-old truth. Being a leader is not easy. Everyone demands something different at different times.

We work in a new world of increasing globalization, ever-changing technology, mass monopolization and a younger generation of workers with new expectations. Leading even the most ambitious of today's workers can be a discouraging task. How do you keep up? How do you be the leader that each of them needs?

One small business owner I work with has found a way to effectively be the chameleon leader he needs to be to get the most of not only his new No. 2s, but his entire staff.

Posted on the wall above his desk at his Twin Cities office is a grid split into four boxes, each representing a number and a corresponding leadership style. It looks something like this:

3. DEVELOPER	2. PROBLEM SOLVER
4. DELEGATOR	1. DIRECTOR

It serves as a visual reminder to him to change his leadership style based on the person, circumstance or time period. More importantly, it's a critical communication tool his employees understand and use to help him better meet their needs. When his employees walk into his office looking for some guidance on a particular task or issue, they point to a window, calling him to respond in a certain leadership style. It's a system that saves time while allowing him to give his employees the clear direction they need.

As John Beck and Neil Yeager say in their book *The Leader's Window*, "Not even the most inexperienced golfer would play using only one kind of club. Nor should leaders aim for foolish consistency using a single leadership style."

Step into the Leader's Window

The four-tiered leadership approach is not a new concept. High-performing teams have relied on this Leadership 4 System described in *The Leader's Window* since the late 80s. The new realities of the working world and global marketplace have led to considerable changes to the L4 System over the past two decades to ensure it remains a valuable communication tool for leaders.

While not a quick fix, the Leader's Window is a methodology owners can use to ensure their approach is effective all the time, every time. With time and practice, owners like my client in the Twin Cities have seen it as a reliable guide for maximizing the potential of employees, particularly No. 2.

Styles 1 and 2 demand leaders to be more directive in their responses while styles 3 and 4 call for a more supportive, listening role. Here's a closer look at how each of the styles play out, as described in *The Leader's Window*:

Style 1: Directing

- High direction
- Leader decides alone
- Requires leader to active influence
- Not dominating

Style 2: Problem Solving

- High support, high direction
- Leader decides with input
- Requires leader to actively listen and influence
- Not over-involved

Style 3: Developing

- High support
- Team member decides with support from leader
- Requires leader to actively listen
- Not over-accommodating

Style 4: Deligating

- Low support, low direction
- Team member decides alone
- Requires leader to not seek or give much information
- Not abdicating

How it Works for No. 2

So what does all this mean when leading No. 2? Well, since No. 2s tend to be high potential individuals, they call leaders to use the 1-4-3-2 sequence when delivering an assignment. This sequence, known as the Empowerment Cycle, calls leaders to keep every window open and use every style with their No. 2s.

3. Developer	2. Problem Solver
4. Delegator	1. Director

How long leaders spend on each style depends on the No. 2's ability to work independently on a given task. The next three steps show how this plays out in any size organization:

Step 1: Give them time to learn and guide them on the path

When No. 2s first moves into the position, it is best to be a director, providing instructions, advice, explanations, and consequences to allow them to do their best work. It's important that leaders encourage their No. 2s to come back with questions and concerns. But do not allow it to spiral out of control with unlimited visits to the office. This style is designed to give No. 2s time to learn about the task and situation so give them direction and then get out of the way.

Upon success, No. 1s can begin to delegate. They can look for opportunities to put their No. 2s in the water and see if they can swim.

The next time you receive a call from a key customer or large account, pass it off. Start by thanking the customer for his ongoing support and then tell him that you are letting "Joe" (your No. 2) take on more responsibility.

"I'm going to share this with him right after I hang up and he'll get back to you with an action plan."

Now, don't stop there. Make sure the customer knows you are still involved and interested in achieving a desirable outcome.

"I'll stay on top of this and if you are not getting the results you want, be sure to call me back."

Recognize this is also a transition for the customer. Show your sensitivity to this by asking for their feedback:

"How do you feel about that?"

This often is challenging for owners who have held the reins so long, but it is critical to securing the future success of the company. This is the first step to bringing a No. 2 into your world and your inner circles of customers and employees.

"Leaders need to deliberately develop their No. 2s by giving them more responsibility over time."

Leaders need to deliberately develop their No. 2s by giving them more responsibility over time. At Bursch Travel, Fred slowly brought Lee into his world, asking her to attend meetings with other travel agency executives, clients, and staff. She met with key customers and as she gradually started to serve their needs, Fred stepped back to allow her to take the reins.

Step 2: Provide them access

With the detailed financial reports in hand, Fred allowed Lee to make some business decisions and when she proved herself as a wise advisor, he promoted her to operations manager. She gained trust among employees who soon looked to her first for guidance. Today, as vice president of the company, Lee handles all of the day-to-day operations, allowing Fred to only visit the corporate office once a week to connect.

But both Fred and Lee will say that reaching that point takes time. It's a transition. Owners have to work to not make decisions for their No. 2s. Encouraging them to take on stretch assignments and then investing the time to develop them is the first step. Lead them through the thinking process by seizing opportunities to ask this series of questions:

- "If I weren't here, from whom would you seek advice?"

- "What steps would you take before making a decision?"

Then ask No. 2 to do the research and take those steps.

Developing a successful No. 2 calls owners to always ask, "What do you think is the right thing to do based on the information you have?" It's more than asking their opinion. It helps them to share what decisions they would make and slowly take on more responsibility. It's essential for not only the success of the No. 2 and the company's daily operations but also the future of the company. It is the basic tenet of preparing a successful plan and positioning the business, and yourself, as an owner, to achieve future goals.

Often, owners shy away from sharing the "insider information" like Fred did for fear that their position is in jeopardy. Beck said it is quite the opposite. Owners actually can stifle their company's growth and their ability to reach their professional and personal goals by failing to cultivate a leader or group of leaders within their organization. "One way to move yourself forward is growing and developing your talent," Beck said.

During my countless meetings with No. 2s, one truth is self-evident: the majority of them do not want the owner's job. They prefer to sit in the No. 2 spot so much that if they were offered the business tomorrow, many admit they would not take it. They do not want the risk or the responsibility. We'll talk more about this in Chapter 7.

Step 3: Be open to changes and new opportunities

This is a process of deliberately developing people and giving them tools to drive your organization – not become you. It's a tough lesson for many owners. Even Beck struggled when he first passed on some of his business responsibilities to a No. 2, his wife. He became frustrated when she did not complete the task as he would have, even if she still received desirable results.

Today, he passes along his experience as he encourages other leaders to not get hung up on having the person do the task just as they have done it. In almost all cases, a No. 2 will not take the exact steps the owner would and that is OK. Many times, the organization is even stronger because of it. Fresh eyes and different outlooks often are healthy for any organization. It's important for owners to recognize that and reinforce their

"If owners are not learning from their No. 2s' progress, they likely are not spending enough time listening."

No. 2s with clear questions, concrete observations and new ideas.

Beck's personal experience with a No. 2 and extensive leadership research have taught him that if owners are not learning from their No. 2s' progress, they likely are not spending enough time listening.

Are you ready?

If you can answer yes to these three questions, you're ready to move forward:

✓ Do I know which leadership style (window) I use most often to teach my No.2?

✓ Do I know when to use the other styles?

✓ Have I committed 1-4-3-2 to memory as a teaching and delegation tool for my No. 2?

Toolbox

Use these tools to get started today. Visit *bigrivergroup.com* or flip to the Appendix for an electronic or printer-friendly versions. Gray indicates tools not yet discussed. Bold indicates tools introduced in this chapter:

Visioning Worksheet
Helps owners transfer their vision to paper and effectively communicate it. (Appendix 1)

Sample Visions
A look at how other No. 1s have put the Visioning Worksheet into practice. (Appendix 2)

Hard Skills'/Soft Skills' Worksheet
Helps owners specify what skills are needed as they search for their No. 2. (Appendix 3)

Resume Review Worksheet
Provides method to identify top candidates for No. 2 job. (Appendix 4)

Email Response Worksheet
Helps evaluate the responses to each emailed question on a three-point scale. (Appendix 5)

Interview Score Sheet
Provides scoring scale to evaluate in-depth questions based on emailed responses. (Appendix 6)

Priorities Worksheet
An owner's guide to articulating a new, perfect destination for their organizations. (Appendix 7)

Priorities to Goals Worksheet
Similar to the Priorities Worksheet, an owner's guide to translating a vision into priorities and goals. (Appendix 8)

Planning Funnel
Provides a planning process to stay on task, increase buy-in and develop a strategic plan that won't gather dust. (Appendix 9)

Outcome Diagnosis Worksheet
A planning tool that helps individuals or a team of individuals identify intended and unintended successes and challenges. (Appendix 10)

Goal Work Plan
A tool to engage a team of employees in creating a well-defined plan of action in less than 30 minutes. (Appendix 11)

My Job, Your Job
Helps translate the owners' vision into priorities and desired outcomes. (Appendix 12)

Employee Feedback Tool
Reinforces the progress of a No. 2 and provides clear, consistent expectations on their roles. (Appendix 13)

Chapter 6

Intentional Progress

"The powerful combination of a visionary No. 1 and a ready-to-go No. 2 can take organizations to great heights."

Overwhelmed, pressed and possibly a little crushed. Those were the sentiments of the staff at St. Cloud Medical Group as it faced mountains of opportunity – and work. With a new clinic administrator and a human resources director, the medical group had aggressive plans to implement a series of electronic medical systems and new technology while improving customer service and physician outreach.

Diana White, the new administrator, had a clear vision of where she wanted to take St. Cloud Medical Group, an independent group of multi-specialty clinics in Central Minnesota (*stcloudmedical.com*). She had ideas for improving operations and was ready to move quickly on key initiatives that related to that vision.

Her energy and the momentum, however, became stifled by "initiative fatigue." The goals were high and the initiatives were many. "We were panicked," said Celeste Gardner, human resources director. "We wondered how we were going to get everything down when we already had full plates."

Celeste, Diana and Patty, chief financial officer, felt they were responsible for every initiative and needed to attend every meeting and be involved in every step. The result: little to no progress.

That changed during a 90-minute session in the medical group's meeting room, and all it took was a blown up spreadsheet on the wall and some directed discussion.

Initative fatigue is a common scenario when visionary No. 1s direct driven No. 2s in organizations of all sizes. The powerful combination of a visionary No. 1 and a ready-to-go No. 2 can take organizations to great heights as long as the vision contains enough details to allow the No. 2 to understand the priorities. No. 1s know what outcomes are the most important to them and the organization, but they often fail to effectively communication them to their No. 2s.

Such failure is not intentional. A lack of communication and proper direction often are caused by one of three scenarios: 1.) No. 1s get too caught up with their own responsibilities, 2.) They focus too much on management of tasks and events and fail to spend enough time on their own vision, or 3.) They don't want to appear pushy, so they stay in Window 4 (as a delegator).

---

5 Steps to Giving an Initiative Legs

1. Owner identifies 3-4 near-term (30-90 day) priorities.
2. Owner writes each priority on the My Job, Your Job poster. (In the first column).
3. Owner identifies one goal per priority and writes that goal on the poster under the priority. (Repeat for each priority/goal).
4. Owner writes names of No. 1, No. 2(s) and key employees or departments across the top row.
5. No. 2s write in what the tasks they will complete for each goal in the column below their respective names.

"The best results from any initiative come when leaders supervise toward outcomes rather than supervising people."

Focus on Outcomes

The best results from any initiative come when leaders supervise toward outcomes rather than supervising people. That requires leaders to focus on upstream efforts. The right efforts will produce the right results. For example, in the Golf My Way DVD, Jack Nicklaus explains how he thinks about and plays the game. Certainly, it does not promise viewers the Masters Championship title. But, at its core, it suggests that by following Nicklaus' swing strategy and understanding his play philosophy, others will achieve positive results.

Owners can take a play from Nicklaus's handbook by forgetting about the organization's broad financial goals for a moment. Instead, owners need to identify expectations and resulting deliverables for the No. 2. If the No. 2 takes care of the action item, then the numbers – those bottom line reports that keep owners up at night – will take care of themselves.

That's not easy for owners to do. When No. 1s become stressed about reaching a specific goal, they can become too focused on the numbers. But the success of a No. 2 requires owners to step back from the numbers when directing their No. 2s and focus on sharing the vision.

As No. 2 starts to achieve some results, owners then need to stand back and let their No. 2 make progress. This will allow the No. 2 to focus on the efforts needed to achieve the vision, which in turn should also achieve the financial benchmarks that are important to owners.

As Nicklaus shows, it's not about controlling the entire two-hundred-plus yards to the target. Instead, Nickalus gets to the hole by controlling the ball over the first six inches. It is the same for No. 1s. They cannot waste time concentrating on every foot of the two hundred yards. Owners need to focus on the first six inches and let the No. 2 take it to the hole.

The My Job, Your Job Worksheet (on page 66 or Appendix 12) helps owners control those critical "first six inches" by translating the owners' vision into priorities and desired outcomes. In as few as 30 minutes, leadership teams can get focused by using the My job, Your Job Worksheet to complete these four steps:

1. Communicate or identify one goal for each of the priorities set by No. 1. (Written in the far left column).
2. Identify one subtask for each goal. (Written under the name of the person who will be completing it).
3. Specify who is responsible for completing each subtask.
4. Set a timeline for completion of each subtask.

My Job, Your Job Worksheet

	Names of Individuals		
Priority 1: Goal:			
Priority 2: Goal:			
Priority 3: Goal:			

"The key to achieving the organization's vision, mission, strategic initiatives and financial goals is to keep the number of priorities low."

Whether it's implementing a new software system or exploring the need for a new vendor in a given area, leaders need to start by identifying the goal. It does not need to be incredibly specific. The goal can be as broad as customer service. The power comes in designing action items and goals tied to the project.

At the medical group, Diana broke down the clinic's lean initiative into a few priorities and identified timeline-driven goals for each priority. For each broad initiative, No. 1s should identify no more than three or four priorities that they want to accomplish. Organizations cannot effectively manage and make progress on more than four priorities. Certainly, as the organization achieves one priority, the owner can identify a new priority so that there are always three to four priorities moving forward in the organization.

The key to achieving the organization's vision, mission, strategic initiatives and financial goals is to keep the number of priorities low, identify only one goal for each of those priorities and provide further clarity by outlining more detailed steps for achieving each of those priorities.

The three to four priorities are expected to be completed within 90 days if possible and certainly no more than six months for medium-size organizations. Smaller organizations with only a few employees should narrow the priorities to no more than three priorities that they want accomplished in the next 30 days.

"No. 1s that focus their vision to only three to four priorities at any given time find that they will accomplish more over the course of a year than they would have if they had identified a dozen."

No. 1s that focus their vision to only three to four priorities at any given time find that they will accomplish more over the course of a year than they would have if they had identified a dozen. Owners can get started and get their No. 2s focused by writing the three to four priorities in the My Job, Your Job Worksheet, on the following page.

My Job, Your Job Worksheet

	Names of Individuals		
Priority 1: Goal:			
Priority 2: Goal:			
Priority 3: Goal:			

Prioritizing the Upstream Steps

At St. Cloud Medical Group, Diana had a vision and three key initiatives she knew would better position the clinic. At first, she tried to stay involved in every part of the initiative and overall operations, as did her No. 2s. Little progress was made. After the initiatives were broken down into priorities and goals for her No. 2s, her vision translated into action and the initiatives took off.

It's essential that leadership teams set specific timelines for each action step. For its e-prescribe priority, the medical group set a date to have hardware in place and another date to complete training. The three women wrote their roles in achieving those goals. Leaders also

"It's more important that the organization gets started on a priority and goal than making detailed plans on achieving them."

can take the My Job, Your Job downstream by committing other staff members to roles within the respective goals.

An owner interested in improving customer service may identify the following priorities:

1. Rewrite performance review tools.
2. Provide manager training regarding underperforming employees.
3. Provide more accurate screening and hiring based on attitude.

This exercise can easily be scaled down to fit the needs of smaller organizations with fewer employees. Growing is an initiative businesses of all sizes and types have in common. A smaller organization interested in growth and expanding its network may identify the following priorities and goals:

Grow and Expand Network

	Names of Individuals		
Priority 1: Increase contact with clients and colleagues. **Goal:** Write and post blogs for leaders in business and education.			
Priority 2: Evaluate pricing of services. **Goal:** Complete a cost analysis for five signature services.			
Priority 3: Expand service footprint. **Goal:** Identify and develop contacts in the four surrounding states.			

For additional insight on how other businesses have used this process, review other completed My Job, Your Job Worksheets in Appendix 12.

If owners aren't careful, they can spend too much time on the details and that can lead to a failure to act. It's more important that the organization gets started on a priority and goal than making detailed plans on achieving them. Although it may increase the owner's anxiety to limit time, the leadership team should spend no more than 30 minutes identifying clear priorities and goals during the session. Success of this part of the session depends on owners taking a hands-on approach and focusing primarily on the first six inches of this drive.

"By nature, a No. 2 is not going to say, 'That's not my job.'"

Once the organization's priorities and goals are identified on the left column of the My Job, Your Job Worksheet and the names of the No. 1, No. 2(s) and other key employees or departments are written across the top row, the worksheet is ready to go to poster size. Leaders can take the worksheet to a local printer, enlarge it to a three-foot by five-foot poster, tape it to a wall in the conference room and call a team meeting.

Drilling Down Deliverables

The management trio at the medical group found focus with a session centered on the My Job, Your Job Worksheet. They came in carrying the responsibility of every initiative and left with only the pieces that related to their jobs and expertise. "By nature, a No. 2 is not going to say, 'That's not my job,'" Patty said. The session gave Patty and Celeste the liberty to step back, pick tasks based on their strengths and experience and, most importantly, not be part of everything. It potentially was a difficult transition for them and Diana. But by focusing only on their piece of the priority and balancing the workload, they could more effectively accomplish the initiatives while successfully completing their other daily tasks.

The My Job, Your Job Worksheet is a great way to foster buy-in and engagement of No. 2 and other key leaders in the organization. The session gives the organization's leaders the opportunity to hear the vision, view the initiatives and then identify how they fit into each priority. In some organizations, the owner or a facilitator actually holds a marker and writes people's tasks on the blown up worksheet. In other organizations, owners hand out markers; and everyone in the room writes where they think they fit into the priorities and goals on the My Job, Your Job Worksheet. Owners with whom I work are often amazed at how quickly their employees take hold of the idea and see their role in making it happen.

Remember, by the time this session is finished, the No. 1 and the No. 2(s) should accomplish the following for each initiative or project:

- Communicate or identify one goal for each of the priorities set by No. 1. (Written in the far left column)

- Identify one subtask for each goal to keep the workload manageable. (Written under the name of the person who will be completing it)
- Specify who is responsible for completing each subtask.
- Set a timeline for completion of each subtask.

No matter how smart, driven and gifted a No. 2 is, No. 1s cannot become hands-off. They still have a responsibility to lead – and supervise – and the best raw material to aid in that supervision is desired outcomes and clear roles. This My Job, Your Job Worksheet exercise provides a quick way to blueprint the organization's vision. As the medical group found, it's impossible to do it all well in a timeframe that achieves revenue goals. But by clearly setting the priorities and goals and distinguishing responsibilities, No. 1 and No. 2 teams can achieve a series of initiatives and position the organization to achieve results today and into the future.

Are you ready?

If you can answer yes to these three questions, you're ready to move forward:

✓ Does my No. 2 understand my vision and can they interpret it clearly for other employees so that those employees understand their roles and responsibilities?

✓ Can I identify three to five near-term priorities and one goal for each one?

✓ Can I blow up the My Job, Your Job Worksheet to 3' by 5' at a local printer?

Toolbox

Use these tools to get started today. Visit *bigrivergroup.com* or flip to the Appendix for an electronic or printer-friendly versions. Gray indicates tools not yet discussed. Bold indicates tools introduced in this chapter:

Visioning Worksheet
Helps owners transfer their vision to paper and effectively communicate it. (Appendix 1)

Sample Visions
A look at how other No. 1s have put the Visioning Worksheet into practice. (Appendix 2)

Hard Skills'/Soft Skills' Worksheet
Helps owners specify what skills are needed as they search for their No. 2. (Appendix 3)

Resume Review Worksheet
Provides method to identify top candidates for No. 2 job. (Appendix 4)

Email Response Worksheet
Helps evaluate the responses to each emailed question on a three-point scale. (Appendix 5)

Interview Score Sheet
Provides scoring scale to evaluate in-depth questions based on emailed responses. (Appendix 6)

Priorities Worksheet
An owner's guide to articulating a new, perfect destination for their organizations. (Appendix 7)

Priorities to Goals Worksheet
Similar to the Priorities Worksheet, an owner's guide to translating a vision into priorities and goals. (Appendix 8)

Planning Funnel
Provides a planning process to stay on task, increase buy-in and develop a strategic plan that won't gather dust. (Appendix 9)

Outcome Diagnosis Worksheet
A planning tool that helps individuals or a team of individuals identify intended and unintended successes and challenges. (Appendix 10)

Goal Work Plan
A tool to engage a team of employees in creating a well-defined plan of action in less than 30 minutes. (Appendix 11)

My Job, Your Job
Helps translate the owners' vision into priorities and desired outcomes. (Appendix 12)

Employee Feedback Tool
Reinforces the progress of a No. 2 and provides clear, consistent expectations on their roles. (Appendix 13)

Chapter 7

Reinforcing Results

If there is one thing that I have learned during my meetings with No. 2s, it's that No. 2s do not want the owner's job. My ears perked up the first time I heard it. I could not believe it. When I heard it repeated time and again, I sat back and had to explore their psyche. The thought of them not desiring to take over the business someday intrigued me, as I am sure it does most business owners. I wanted to better understand what it takes to reinforce these high-potential individuals and, as we'll talk about later in the book, how to keep them.

"I treat this company like I own it, but I don't want to own it. I really don't."

- Lee Hurd, No. 2 at Bursh Travel

No matter the organization size, No. 2s openly shared that they did not take the No. 2 position because they have goals of moving into the No. 1 spot or leading their own business one day. Serving as No. 2 – and working closely with the owner – only solidified those sentiments. "I treat this company like I own it, but I don't want to own it. I really don't," said Lee Hurd, a longtime No. 2 at Bursch Travel.

As business owners who have a natural tendency to create, grow and own something with our name on it, it's hard to understand why people would take on the responsibility and not want what we see as the reward. Although No. 2s recognize that ownership comes with its rewards, they are not interested in the risk. They do not want to go home at night and worry about how they're going to keep the doors open through tough economic times, like the times Bursch Travel experienced the months following the attacks of 9/11. They know owners carry a lot on their shoulders and it's a burden they would rather live without. "I don't want to have to think like an owner," Lee said. "I don't want to lay awake at night thinking about what to do."

Lee has great compassion for the employees at Bursch Travel and would do anything to support them. I am sure she has worried about the staff in her off-hours. She cares about them, and they know it. But at the end of the day, she is thankful that Fred Bursch is the person who needs to step up to the plate – and he has.

After 9/11, he was willing to take out a second mortgage on his home to ensure that he could make payroll and avoid layoffs during the devastating downturn in the travel industry. His actions following 9/11 and during countless other challenges and opportunities have demonstrated his leadership and made him a person Lee is proud to work alongside as the No. 2.

Successful No. 2s are highly talented individuals and often are sought after by other organizations – no matter the economic conditions. Retaining No. 2s is dependent upon reinforcing them. That includes owners communicating the significant role the No. 2 plays in the organization's success and the professional growth opportunities in the organization that they have in mind for their No. 2s.

"No. 2s, overachievers by nature, thrive on most of the feedback they receive from their No. 1s."

Step 1: Conduct regular feedback sessions and reviews

Effectively reinforcing No. 2s starts with conducting regular feedback sessions and performance reviews. No. 2s, overachievers by nature, thrive on most of the feedback they receive from their No. 1s. They treat the organization as their own and want to know how they can better lead the company to the desired destination.

Fostering the best performance from No. 2s requires frequent and consistent feedback, but it does not need to be as formal as a paper performance review. These feedback sessions and performance reviews cannot be just another task on the to-do list for any employee, particularly results-driven No. 2s. Owners need to resist the temptation to provide drive-by supervision when a quality lunch with focused conversation can foster measurable progress.

It may not be a long lunch hour with the No. 2, but owners need to invest time in creating a format that allows them to effectively deliver key information to their

No. 2s in terms of mastering key skills, meeting job responsibilities and achieving goals that are aligned with the organization's vision and overall strategic plan.

Owners can leverage performance reviews to not only measure a No. 2s performance and progress, but also identify goals and create an action plan to more effectively achieve those goals in the coming months and year. That may include building skills in a given area to allow them to take on more responsibility and grow within the organization. Owners need to identify specific indicators of success and include these metrics in the performance review to allow them and their No. 2s to track progress and identify growth areas.

This ongoing improvement plan – and corresponding dialogue between owners and their No. 2s – cannot be achieved in just one annual review. The first reason stems from human nature and an employee's anticipation of the raise, a common reward for a job well done. During annual reviews, employees typically are listening for the raise so much so that it clouds their ability to absorb other constructive feedback. They inevitably tune out the true substance of the review: the goals and action steps. The infrequency of annual reviews also makes it challenging for the owner to set a clear direction for the No. 2 and make adjustments in a time frame that optimizes results.

More frequent feedback sessions, often conducted quarterly, help No. 2s make more focused progress throughout the year. They also provide concrete examples of key accomplishments on particular projects and other information that owners can use to provide a more detailed annual review.

Owners find that spending time throughout the year pays off at year's end, and annual reviews practically write themselves. The result is a richer annual review; plus, by the time the No. 2s meet with the owner, they know what to expect. There should not be any surprises in reviews no matter when they are given. It's important that the owner does not wait for annual reviews or yearly feedback sessions to communicate key issues. This will stifle progress and leave No. 2s wondering where else they may be going wrong.

"While this tool would work with almost any employee, it is a key to reinforcing the progress of a No. 2 and providing clear, consistent expectations on their roles."

Owners can better direct the discussion by using the Employee Feedback Tool (Appendix 13). While this tool would work with almost any employee, it is a key to reinforcing the progress of a No. 2 and providing clear, consistent expectations on their roles. The tool is broken down into three areas: company goals, personal goals and other performance.

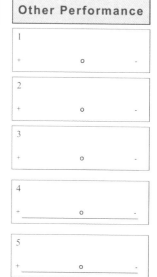

Under the first column on company goals, owners should write down the three to four priorities and goals outlined using the My Job, Your Job or Goal Benchmark Worksheets from Chapter 6. This column will only change when the company's priorities change.

For the second column, owners and No. 2s use the company goals to set personal goals for the No. 2. In each of the three boxes, No. 2s write three specific, short-term goals that are connected to the company's vision. At the feedback session, owners circle the plus, zero, or minus symbols under each personal goal to quickly communicate progress and improvement areas.

Under the third and final column, No. 1s can write other performance examples they noticed since the last feedback session. This facilitates specific feedback on successes or challenges. An owner could write how they witnessed the No. 2's leadership at an all-staff meeting to kick-off a new initiative or the growth in a specific vendor relationship. It's important to identify the high points and low points in the No. 2's performance and then evaluate them, using the plus, zero and minus scale.

While the owner's grade provides a powerful cue to No. 2s at the performance review or feedback session, it

"Effective reviews also allow No. 2s to evaluate their performance in the same key areas and give themselves a grade."

is not the only grade that is important. Effective reviews also allow No. 2s to evaluate their performance in the same key areas and give themselves a grade. Owners need to ask the No. 2s to return the self-review before the face-to-face review meeting to allow owners time to read and reflect on the No. 2s' responses. By knowing how No. 2s feel about their performance and which areas they would like to focus on improving, owners can feel more at ease when conducting the formalized performance review.

Step 2: Leverage compensation plans

Sure, grades are important. Just as when we received an "A" in the fifth grade, we were also interested in the recognition that followed. We would sit in our desks, trying not to beam with excitement when the teacher sung our praises. I still remember the look on my daughters' faces when we rewarded their accomplishment with some prime real estate on our refrigerator for others

"From stars for learning to go to the bathroom to pizza parties for reading the most books in class, society has made us accustomed to receiving rewards for performance."

to see. From stars for learning to go to the bathroom to pizza parties for reading the most books in class, society has made us accustomed to receiving rewards for performance.

Those refrigerator days are a distant memory for most No. 2s but they still appreciate a reward, most often found in compensation plans. Corporate America has long embraced compensation as a key tool in attracting and retaining executives. But many would agree these compensations plans have been used to pad executive pockets, not fuel the company's bottom lines. The names of the Fortune 500 companies in the newspaper headlines change, but the premise remains the same. The company is under-performing, its share price is trailing and the top executives receive big raises. The problem: the company is not paying for performance.

Most organizations understand that compensation plans are powerful tools in retaining and attracting talent. Typically, salary and benefits are communicated to a prospective employee early on. Still, compensation plans are underutilized because few organizations recognize the impact these plans can have on driving success for the employee and the organization.

"When crafted correctly, compensation plans serve as a powerful tool that focuses No. 2s on key goals and reinforces them for achievement."

When crafted correctly, compensation plans serve as a powerful tool that focuses No. 2s on key goals and reinforces them for achievement. Dollars are tangible and have a clear value for employees in terms of a paycheck, but compensation plans should not be just about the salary. Paid time off, healthcare benefits and a rising salary only break the surface of competitive compensation packages that motivate No. 2s.

Mike McCarty, a human resource and management consultant with 30 years of experience working with organizations, said creating effective compensation plans requires businesses to think outside of the box. That may include providing hardware incentives through laptops, Internet access at home, cell phones, company cars and other materials that employees need to do their jobs.

Other businesses take compensation plans a step farther by investing in what the business world has coined "key man insurance." This unconventional insurance policy, sometimes called the "golden handcuff," solidifies loyalty by delivering No. 2s a sizable payout if they stay with the organization for a set number of years, typically at least 15 years. The policy sends a clear message to No. 2s: they are valued and the organization needs them to thrive in the next 10 or 20 years.

"The more creative the compensation plans the more effective they are in getting the No. 2's attention and promoting desired outcomes."

The more creative the compensation plans the more effective they are in getting the No. 2's attention and promoting desired outcomes. While it's easy to pull an idea from the headlines, owners can position their No. 2s and business for lasting success by taking the time to evaluate their options and creating compensation plans that are connected to organizational benchmarks.

At the core of any effective compensation plan is a competitive salary. This allows the organization to attract and retain quality talent. "It doesn't need to be more (than your competitors)," Mike said. "It can be less. It just needs to be in the ballpark." Then, reinforce the No. 2 through additional rewards based on measurable outcomes.

A common example is commission for sales professionals. They receive a certain percentage or another monetary value for each product or series of products they sell. While this has fostered some results in the sales sector for decades, it only begins to leverage a compensation plan. It promotes more sales, but often does not pinpoint how the individuals should achieve more volume for the company.

A new salesman could be at the top of the sales performance chart for the month because he can make a quick sale. But his sales methods do not foster return business like the salesman who ranks No. 3 on the list. The No. 1 salesman only delivers a short-term gain. In most cases, companies prefer building relationships that

"Business owners who measure quantity, quality, money and time will better measure a No. 2's performance."

foster return business. In the end, a salesman like No. 3 who builds relationships will allow the company to direct fewer resources into marketing their products, so No. 3 likely could be more profitable for the company in the long-term, even though he doesn't have the highest volume month-to-month.

This direct sales model also fails to apply to No. 2s who are working on long-term projects. Astute business owners can take this reinforcement model a step farther by tying a specific organizational goal to four key benchmarks, instead of on money. Business owners who measure quantity, quality, money and time will better measure a No. 2's performance. Here's a look at the breakdown and applications of these benchmarks:

1. **Quantity:** State a concrete goal, typically tied to a number.

   Example: The organization will increase membership sales by 30 percent over three years.

2. **Quality:** Identify actions to achieve the quantitative goal.

   Example: Today, members use the services once a week. The No. 2 will add three strategic programs aimed at providing value and increasing utilization to three times a week.

3. **Money:** Tie the quantitative goal to a monetary gain.

   Example: The No. 2 will translate a 30 percent in membership to a 30 percent increase in revenue.

4. **Time:** Break a long-term goal into intermediate steps that are manageable and measurable.

   Example: Increase membership 5 percent the first year, 10 percent the second year and 15 percent the third year for a total increase of 30 percent over three years.

While compensation plans are only limited by the owner's imagination, plans that are tied to progress, performance and even effort encourage proper risk taking and lead No. 2s to provide organizations with their best performance during times of change.

Step 3: Reward with quality time

Above all, No. 2s desire the owner's most prized possession: the owner's time. Setting aside a long lunch every two weeks with No. 2s will go a long way in reinforcing their efforts, tracking their progress and, most importantly, celebrating their successes. For each meeting, No. 1s need to ask their No. 2s to bring an agenda and possibly even attach a number from the Leader's Window, outlined in Chapter 5, to signal what leadership style they need from the owner in each area.

Owners will achieve the best results by staying on the macro-level. This challenges No. 1s to ask their No. 2s to ask "how" questions, rather than the common "why" ones. Faced with a new project, this approach calls No. 2s to ask for direction through a question like "If your vision is to increase membership by 30 percent, how do you want me to handle…?" It also provides a growth opportunity for No. 2s. Owners can easily build their No. 2s' self esteem and confidence by giving them challenges and rewarding them when they succeed.

Their way may not be the owner's way. But that's OK and it still may be the "right" way. Celebrate free-thinking because bringing in a No. 2 is not about creating a clone of the owner.

Undermining a No. 2's initiative or micromanaging the project is demoralizing and can stifle the No. 2's progress and the organization's bottom line. Owners need to embrace risk for the sake of the future growth of the No. 2. If owners cannot bear the thought of allowing their No. 2s to make their own mistakes, their No. 2s will never reach their potential and neither will the organization.

Above all, effective reinforcement requires owners to be intentional. Taking a haphazard approach almost inevitably will lead to missed opportunities to develop a No. 2 and, thereby, missing an opportunity to grow the business.

Are you ready?

If you can answer yes to these three questions, you're ready to move forward:

✓ Can I identify 3-4 essential priorities per quarter?

✓ Can I identify what I want my No. 2 to accomplish for each priority? (Refer to the My Job, Your Job Worksheet from Chapter 6, if necessary).

✓ Do I schedule quality time (not drive-by) to review and reinforce progress of my No. 2?

Toolbox

Use these tools to get started today. Visit *bigrivergroup.com* or flip to the Appendix for an electronic or printer-friendly versions. Gray indicates tools not yet discussed. Bold indicates tools introduced in this chapter:

Visioning Worksheet
Helps owners transfer their vision to paper and effectively communicate it. (Appendix 1)

Sample Visions
A look at how other No. 1s have put the Visioning Worksheet into practice. (Appendix 2)

Hard Skills'/Soft Skills' Worksheet
Helps owners specify what skills are needed as they search for their No. 2. (Appendix 3)

Resume Review Worksheet
Provides method to identify top candidates for No. 2 job. (Appendix 4)

Email Response Worksheet
Helps evaluate the responses to each emailed question on a three-point scale. (Appendix 5)

Interview Score Sheet
Provides scoring scale to evaluate in-depth questions based on emailed responses. (Appendix 6)

Priorities Worksheet
An owner's guide to articulating a new, perfect destination for their organizations. (Appendix 7)

Priorities to Goals Worksheet
Similar to the Priorities Worksheet, an owner's guide to translating a vision into priorities and goals. (Appendix 8)

Planning Funnel
Provides a planning process to stay on task, increase buy-in and develop a strategic plan that won't gather dust. (Appendix 9)

Outcome Diagnosis Worksheet
A planning tool that helps individuals or a team of individuals identify intended and unintended successes and challenges. (Appendix 10)

Goal Work Plan
A tool to engage a team of employees in creating a well-defined plan of action in less than 30 minutes. (Appendix 11)

My Job, Your Job
Helps translate the owners' vision into priorities and desired outcomes. (Appendix 12)

Employee Feedback Tool
Reinforces the progress of a No. 2 and provides clear, consistent expectations on their roles. (Appendix 13)

Chapter 8

Getting Beyond the Blunders

"Be hard on the problem and easy on the people."

It often starts the same way. Drive-by owners spout off a long list of to dos or thoughts to their No. 2 and intend on touching base later. But time gets away and by the time they reconnect, their No. 2 is floundering, the project has gone astray or the No. 2 has a made a mistake that requires the owner's time and attention. This can make owners question if they had made the right decision when choosing their No. 2 or wonder if anyone will be able to really be a No. 2 and help grow the organization.

Owners need to put those worries aside. Mistakes will happen. They are a part of the process of grooming a No. 2 and positioning the organization for smart growth. But for many owners who are accustomed to holding the reins on their own, this is unchartered territory and will require some learning along the way.

If there is one piece of advice I'd like owners to remember, it would be to be hard on the problem and easy on the people. This will prevent mistakes from completely stifling the project at hand. When a mistake happens, it's best to say "Wow, that didn't work," and move on to prevent cutting off conversation, participation and future progress.

Stay away from subjective comments about inadequacy. No, it is not always easy. It takes practice. Owners need to be very intentional with their words and actions to overcome the mistake and help their No. 2 learn from it. Successful No. 1s focus on providing an objective analysis of the problem and offering possible solutions. Instead of pointing fingers when someone drops the ball during a project, they ask questions like "Do we need to know more about our market? What additional information would have been helpful to know about our vendor before deciding?" Here are some practical leadership techniques to get the No. 2 back on track and performing to the owner's expectations:

Step 1: Practice the one-minute manager

Owners can use their time more effectively by managing in one minute. Yes, it is possible. The one-minute manager technique, developed by Ken Blanchard, has long been used in high-performing organizations, and I have seen it produce results for many owners with whom I work. The one-minute manager is grounded in the implementation of the three key steps:

1. **One-minute goals:** Establish clear-cut goals.

2. **One-minute praise:** Recognize good performance.

3. **One-minute improvement:** Reprimand when performance fails to support common goals.

So how do owners turn that into action in their organizations? Like I said, it takes practice. Most owners already practice these steps in one form or another. They just need to refine their approach slightly.

No. 1s can start with clear-cut goals. All good performance is based on goals that are understandable and

"All good performance is based on goals that are understandable and measurable."

measurable. No. 2s want to meet – and exceed – the owners' expectations. It's the owner's job to set them up for success with a roadmap.

Astute No. 1s keep it simple by limiting the number of goals to three to five on any project. That will allow both the owner and No. 2 to keep them on top of their minds and moving forward. Owners need to see this as a partnership and agree on the goals upfront. For Tara Tollefson, CEO of The Buzz Company, bringing in a No. 2 was necessary to meet an increasing demand for company's customer relations services and grow the business. Like many owners, she had worn all the hats and deciding which ones to hand off to a No. 2 required some thought and strategy.

Tara played to her new No. 2's strengths of communication, organization and video production. Pam Nelson organized her "buzz group" meetings and compiled the feedback in a clear format that Tara could analyze for her clients. Pam also brought exceptional video storytelling skills to the business, giving Tara an opportunity to expand the company's line of marketing services. Tara took it slow to see how "buzz videos" would enhance her offerings and not detract from the company's core services.

It worked. Videos became a strong selling point for The Buzz Company and heightened demand for the company's services. Tara greeted the success with praise – privately and publicly – for Pam. The success of grooming a No. 2 lies in catching that person doing something positive. No one likes sea gull managers that fly in, make some racket, dump on everyone and then fly out.

If there is one thing I have learned from my countless meetings with No. 2s, it's that a "Good Job," "Well done" or "Thank you" goes a long way. Often, owners do not say those simple lines enough. But, they shouldn't stop there. Detailed praise goes even farther.

Successful No. 1s deliver compliments on a specific task or project. When No. 2s lead a client meeting well, motivate an employee or improve a process, owners need to tell them why it was a job well done. This not only provides motivation, but also direction. Praising progress even when it is minimal gives No. 2s the fuel to keep moving the organization forward and not left wondering if they are doing the right thing.

Remember, No. 2s are still learning, so when they make a mistake, No. 1s should respond quickly. The owner's first response needs to be redirection. No. 1s need to hold their No. 2 accountable, but never punish a learner. That will immobilize the No. 2 and stifle the organization's success. Owners can take a breath and then take a minute to advise their No. 2 on one of the following:

1. What does the No. 1 want

OR

2. What was done incorrectly

OR

3. How to do it

While it may be human nature to do all three at once, it's critical that owners only choose one to accomplish in a minute and stay on message. Owners can keep a dialogue going by sharing some information and then asking if their No. 2 needs more on that. That may translate into owners saying, "In the future, when dealing with a customer, do these three steps..." or "When you work

"It is critical that owners only choose one to accomplish in a minute and stay on message."

with our top customers, don't ever do...." Successful leaders keep it clear, succinct and objective.

Step 2: Re-delegate as needed

There will be times when owners will need to step back and re-delegate the task. This often happens when No. 2 comes to the owner and wants to know how to do better or asks for more direction on the long-term vision. These situations suggest the possibility that the owner did not spend enough time on the front end to provide the proper direction and now needs to invest the time. Still, re-delegating a task does not mean the No. 2 or owner failed. It is part of the grooming and learning process.

At Bursch Travel, when Lee did not fully understand Fred's vision, she struggled to achieve the results she wanted and Fred desired. They both were frustrated. But once they stepped back and Fred fully outlined his 5-year vision on paper, Lee understood where Fred wanted the agency to go and her role in helping him achieve it.

When situations like this arise, owners need to return to the Leader's Window, but this time, and use 1-4-3-2, known as the Development or Empowerment Cycle. This sequence calls leaders to keep every window open – direct, problem solve, develop and delegate: use every style with their No. 2s. Through this cycle, owners provide No. 2s with clear assignments and frequent checkpoints. Owners need to start by telling their No. 2s what they want from their No. 2, then set a specific deadline to meet again or let No. 2 decide when to check in to track progress.

This is not easy for owners because of their tendency to want to solve the problem. That spirit is one of the assets that make them successful entrepreneurs. But when grooming a No. 2, owners need to think of themselves as "Yoda" and guide No. 2 to the solution.

Step 3: Motivate a procrastinator

Everyone procrastinates now and again on a task that seems too large, too tedious or too difficult to tackle at that point. It's human nature. But when owners find themselves going from Window No. 1 to No. 4 and then back to No. 1 to No. 4 and so on, it's affecting the organization's success and it's time to step in. Owners are most successful in overcoming procrastination paralysis of their No. 2s by focusing on Leader's Window No. 2. This requires them to provide high levels of support and direction.

"No. 1s can begin by breaking the task into three steps that can be monitored and follow the Rule of 3 to establish checkpoints."

No. 1s can begin by breaking the task into three steps that can be monitored and follow the Rule of 3 to establish checkpoints. For the first two steps, owners need to tell their No. 2 specifically when they would like to hear the results of the given assigned task. For the third and final step of the task, owners *ask* their No. 2 to come to them with the results. Here's how it can play out:

"Joe, I would like you to (insert step 1). It is 10 minutes to 3 now. I'm going to stop by your desk just before 4 p.m. and I'd like to see this task completed. Tomorrow, by 9 a.m., I'd like to talk to you about what you found

out on (step 2). By 11 a.m., you come to me with the results of (step 3)."

Procrastinators tend to stall major decisions in hopes that they will go away. Procrastinators avoid making decisions with a stalling strategy to compromise between being honest and not hurting anyone. Owners can more effectively get results by identifying what the procrastinator's real concerns are, help them solve their problems with a decision and retain control over the action steps.

Step 4: Outside coaching

While the leadership, wisdom and insight of owners make them the best people to guide and groom No. 2s, owners should not carry it all on their shoulders. Investing in outside coaching is a valuable performance tool that can turn around underperformers and propel strong performers to the next level.

High-performing organizations do not make coaching an improvisational affair or take the on-the-fly leadership approach. Instead, they make coaching a part of the orientation and on-boarding process. Outside coaches can facilitate the process, set parameters, create an action plan and measure results. Harvard Management Studies cite these three key coaching methods to use:

1. Address specific development area, such as delegating more effectively.
2. Prepare a manager to take on a new role (such as a No. 2).
3. Support an individual in handling an exceptional management challenge, such as leading a new effort.

Outside coaches bring valuable objectivity to the development process. They measure results through a before and after assessment and give owners and No. 2s the 360-degree feedback they both desire.

Influence

Mistakes will happen, but many can be avoided by taking some strategic steps that boil down to owners using their influence to achieve results. Owners are most successful when they understand it's their responsibility to communicate the vision and direct their No. 2 toward identifying and taking the necessary action steps to achieve it.

Leaders who effectively influence their No. 2s produce lasting results by not only helping them to improve, but also showing them how to encourage other staff to reach their potential. No. 1s set the example for their No. 2s to use when developing people in their organization. If No. 1s fail in this, then, they may be setting up their No. 2 for mistakes.

Are you ready?

If you can answer yes to these three questions, you're ready to move forward:

✓ Am I able to remove blame and emotion when talking to my No. 2s about their mistakes?

✓ Can I move smoothly through the 1-4-3-2 Development Cycle with my No. 2?

✓ Have I made the necessary changes and improvements to the My Job, Your Job Worksheet to ensure it is effectively directing my No. 2s?

Toolbox

Use these tools to get started today. Visit *bigrivergroup.com* or flip to the Appendix for an electronic or printer-friendly versions. Gray indicates tools not yet discussed. Bold indicates tools introduced in this chapter:

Visioning Worksheet
Helps owners transfer their vision to paper and effectively communicate it. (Appendix 1)

Sample Visions
A look at how other No. 1s have put the Visioning Worksheet into practice. (Appendix 2)

Hard Skills'/Soft Skills' Worksheet
Helps owners specify what skills are needed as they search for their No. 2. (Appendix 3)

Resume Review Worksheet
Provides method to identify top candidates for No. 2 job. (Appendix 4)

Email Response Worksheet
Helps evaluate the responses to each emailed question on a three-point scale. (Appendix 5)

Interview Score Sheet
Provides scoring scale to evaluate in-depth questions based on emailed responses. (Appendix 6)

Priorities Worksheet
An owner's guide to articulating a new, perfect destination for their organizations. (Appendix 7)

Priorities to Goals Worksheet
Similar to the Priorities Worksheet, an owner's guide to translating a vision into priorities and goals. (Appendix 8)

Planning Funnel
Provides a planning process to stay on task, increase buy-in and develop a strategic plan that won't gather dust. (Appendix 9)

Outcome Diagnosis Worksheet
A planning tool that helps individuals or a team of individuals identify intended and unintended successes and challenges. (Appendix 10)

Goal Work Plan
A tool to engage a team of employees in creating a well-defined plan of action in less than 30 minutes. (Appendix 11)

My Job, Your Job
Helps translate the owners' vision into priorities and desired outcomes. (Appendix 12)

Employee Feedback Tool
Reinforces the progress of a No. 2 and provides clear, consistent expectations on their roles. (Appendix 13)

CHAPTER 9

THINKING LIKE OWNERS

Imagine if every employee in an organization started thinking like an owner. Imagine if employees shared the owner's beliefs, understood the vision and focused their energy on making the business successful. How would it affect customer service calls, sales, profits and the overall spirit of the company? Without a doubt, it would push companies to a higher level of professionalism, profit and employee excellence.

Even the employees of e-commerce giant *Amazon. com* have not forgotten to think like owners. Employees at one of the company's fulfillment centers in Kentucky delivered energy savings to the company by unscrewing the light bulbs in their cafeteria's vending machines. After recognizing the bottom line savings, Amazon made it a company-wide policy and now saves $20,000 a year on electricity.

Southwest Airlines (*southwestairlines.com*) entrusts employees to keep the "Southwest Spirit" alive and makes them feel as though they can make decisions on the company's behalf. It's what Fred Taylor, SWA manager of proactive customer communications, says makes Southwest's customer service unique and earned it an exceptional reputation in the industry.

While a culture of ownership must run throughout the organization, it can start with the No. 2. The more successful the No. 2, the faster the company can grow. Time and again, I have seen dynamite No. 2s drive progress and help organizations grow. The common denominator is the No. 2's ability to think like an owner.

While compensation (as we talked about in Chapter 7) can help instill an ownership mentality in a No. 2, it only begins to harness a No. 2's intellect and ingenuity for the good of the organization. When No. 2s think like owners, they consistently make decisions in the best interest of the company, its customers and employees. They are nimble, can respond to adversity and do what it takes to achieve the vision.

Often, it is easy for No. 1s to see the big picture and maybe even find a No. 2 with the passion, skills and personality needed to fulfill the organization's vision. But

---

Does Your No. 2 Have What It Takes?

Here are six qualities found in successful entrepreneurs that also translate to thriving No. 2s:

1. Innovative
2. Results-oriented
3. Self-motivated
4. Driven to accomplish tasks
5. Open to change
6. Self-confident

---

the successful integration of a No. 2 takes more than a company orientation or week-long job shadow. It needs to be intentional and it needs to start immediately. So, here are three steps that any owner can use to empower a No. 2 to think – and act – like an owner:

Step 1: Explain big-picture to your No. 2

No. 2s cannot have a one-dimensional view of their role in the company. They cannot see themselves as the director of sales, executive vice president or chief financial officer. Those are job titles. Ask owners their job title and they will either rattle off a series or pause in search of the words to describe their role in the company. No. 2s should offer a similar response.

"Making sure the No. 2 understands the company's vision is the first step to getting them to think like an owner."

Getting No. 2s to think like owners requires No. 1s to come alongside and encourage them to think beyond their job description or their department to gain a complete business view. They may handle human resources, for example, but they may also need to understand the financial picture and the future of products or services. Leaders cannot allow any No. 2 from operating in a silo. From sales and billing to product development and marketing, owners need to show their No. 2s how the entire business operates and communicate where it is headed. Owners are big-picture people, but that does not mean their No. 2s don't need to be. Making sure the No. 2 understands the company's vision is the first step to getting them to think like an owner.

Giving a No. 2 a big-picture of the organization requires owners to communicate the key items frequently on every owner's mind:

- Customer Experience
- Marketing

- Revenue

- Staff Development

- Leadership Structure

Owners will see a greater return on their investment if they take time – often – to share with their No. 2s what they think about these big-picture items and help the No. 2 keep them top of mind.

Step 2: Make No. 2s vision-oriented

Sharing vision is essential to achieving it. Owners cannot do it alone and their top ally is their No. 2. Leaders will accomplish their company goals faster – and even go farther – if they effectively engage their No. 2 in delivering the vision downstream in the organization.

As we've talked about throughout this book, owners need to invest time in communicating their vision to their No. 2. Put it on paper (use the tools in Chapter 4 to articulate the vision). Although they wish they could, No. 2s cannot read owner's minds. They need the vision on paper so that they can see their place in it and help the organization achieve it. Once a vision is in place, owners need to encourage their No. 2 to also clearly articulate what talents and skills they can bring to the process and how they will achieve the vision.

Once the vision is understood, No. 2s need to share it. Owners cannot be the only people communicating the vision. No. 2s, typically self-motivated and driven by nature, can be the owner's vision ambassadors and help communicate the vision to employees at varying levels in the organization. Today, Fred Bursch spends little time in each office. But he clearly articulated a vision that his No. 2, Lee, can share with managers and employees and use as a gauge to ensure the organization remains on the right track, whether Fred is there or not. With the vision in mind, Lee does not need to wonder "What would Fred do?" She already knows the answer.

Successful No. 1s communicate their vision in terms of both an ideal organization and ideal products or services. An ideal organizational vision may be as simple as being known as the best restaurant in town or becoming a top 10 university. The vision for ideal products and services can be equally as straightforward: providing the best customer service or producing flawless widgets at a reasonable cost. The specific action steps and strategy needed to achieve the vision is what makes the paper powerful to the No. 2.

"Teach that 'owner impulse' to No. 2s by encouraging them to relate every project and every decision back to the vision."

No. 2s who understand the big, even lofty, vision for the organization can more effectively direct the company's resources and employees' attention. Thinking like an owner means linking every action back to the vision. Teach that "owner impulse" to No. 2s by encouraging them to relate every project and every decision back to the vision. As a reflex, No. 2s need to respond to a question from an employee or a new opportunity with a vendor by asking themselves "How will this move the vision forward?"

Every good No. 2 is also a diplomat. No. 2s need to be able to manage the needs of No. 1s while keeping their fellow employees productive and generally happy. No. 2s are ambassadors inside the organization not only because they have detailed information on the vision but also because they set the tone in the organization. Other employees look to the No. 2 to determine how they should react to a situation. In many cases, No. 2s become a staff liaison – effectively communicating the owner's wishes while securing employee trust and

"A great No. 2 already knows what needs to be done and then does it."

- Lee Hurd, Bursh Travel No. 2

confidence that some owners may not generate. In some ways, I've seen No. 2s serve almost as a den mother or den father. They help both owners and employees talk through issues and challenges as well as offer options and content for future actions.

Step 3: Give them freedom

Most No. 2s have a great ability to listen and learn. That's what makes them the people owners depend on day in and day out. When given the liberty, No. 2s will do what Lee does at Bursch. They will remove the obstacles, leverage the resources and find new ways to achieve the owner's vision. "A great No. 2 already knows what needs to be done and then does it," Lee said. No. 2s thrive on that success and making the owner proud.

Leaders give their No. 2s freedom by using Leader's Window No. 4 (from Chapter 4). Astute owners practice the art of delegation by allowing No. 2s to review the facts and make a decision. This includes looking at the tasks on to the to-do list and prioritizing them. It's important that leaders deliberately develop their No. 2s by giving them more responsibility over time and to plan sub-steps for the initiatives.

This will provide No. 2s with a sense of significance. They will feel as though their contributions matter and, more importantly, feel like they are helping to drive the vision. By encouraging increased responsibility and trust, organizations begin to create a culture of ownership for their No. 2s and every other employee.

Leaders who empower their No. 2s through regular, meaningful interaction will find that they not only get more results from their No. 2 but also the entire team. Just as the No. 2 looks to an owner's example, other employees in the organization look to the No. 2 to set the tone and expectations and identify specific action steps.

At Heartland Glass Company (*heartlandglass.com*), owner Bill Sullivan gave one of most promising employees the freedom to become a part of the vision. Even before Ryan Torgerson officially assumed the No. 2 spot, he started thinking like an owner. Ryan's ownership mentality led him to take some strategic steps to improve the health and vitality of the organization. Here are just a few of the steps that earned him a No. 2 spot:

1. Identified about a dozen things the company could do to be even more successful and then brought his ideas to the owner.

2. Helped show the owners what decisions needed to be made.

3. Offered suggestions on what the owner could delegate.

4. Gently moved the vision forward.

5. Played a pivotal role in sharing the vision within the company.

6. Demonstrated need for a No. 2 spot in the company.

Ryan's smart moves and gentle guidance led Bill to create a No. 2 spot in the organization for Ryan. Bill now relies on Ryan to pick up and complete tasks without a word said. It's a smooth partnership that allows each of them to use their insight and experience to make Heartland stronger and more successful.

Even owners have a lot to learn. It's not easy running – and growing – a successful operation. It's even harder to let go of the day-to-day responsibilities and give

"Wise No. 1s can receive coaching-level feedback from their No. 2s and find ways to encourage it."

others some control over operation and outcomes. But those business owners who have the courage to take on a No. 2 and give that person some freedom in the organization will see the return in higher morale, increased revenue and better customer service. Two brains are better than one. Wise No. 1s can receive coaching-level feedback from their No. 2s and find ways to encourage it.

Coaching Up

Did you realize that frequently asked questions by No. 2s are essentially coaching for No. 1s? Here are a few tips No. 2s can use to effectively coach their No. 1s:

- Plan what to say. What are the key points of the conversation?
- Practice the conversation in your mind.
- Deliver your key points and then allow the owner to reflect.
- Reinforce the key statement or message.
- Clearly define any next steps.

Are you ready?

If you can answer yes to these three questions, you're ready to move forward:

✓ Have I put my vision for the organization on paper for my No. 2?

✓ Have I developed a No. 2 that thinks like an owner?

✓ Have I empowered and entrusted my No. 2 to feel like he/she can make decisions on behalf of the company?

Toolbox

Use these tools to get started today. Visit *bigrivergroup.com* or flip to the Appendix for an electronic or printer-friendly versions. Gray indicates tools not yet discussed. Bold indicates tools introduced in this chapter:

Visioning Worksheet
Helps owners transfer their vision to paper and effectively communicate it. (Appendix 1)

Sample Visions
A look at how other No. 1s have put the Visioning Worksheet into practice. (Appendix 2)

Hard Skills'/Soft Skills' Worksheet
Helps owners specify what skills are needed as they search for their No. 2. (Appendix 3)

Resume Review Worksheet
Provides method to identify top candidates for No. 2 job. (Appendix 4)

Email Response Worksheet
Helps evaluate the responses to each emailed question on a three-point scale. (Appendix 5)

Interview Score Sheet
Provides scoring scale to evaluate in-depth questions based on emailed responses. (Appendix 6)

Priorities Worksheet
An owner's guide to articulating a new, perfect destination for their organizations. (Appendix 7)

Priorities to Goals Worksheet
Similar to the Priorities Worksheet, an owner's guide to translating a vision into priorities and goals. (Appendix 8)

Planning Funnel
Provides a planning process to stay on task, increase buy-in and develop a strategic plan that won't gather dust. (Appendix 9)

Outcome Diagnosis Worksheet
A planning tool that helps individuals or a team of individuals identify intended and unintended successes and challenges. (Appendix 10)

Goal Work Plan
A tool to engage a team of employees in creating a well-defined plan of action in less than 30 minutes. (Appendix 11)

My Job, Your Job
Helps translate the owners' vision into priorities and desired outcomes. (Appendix 12)

Employee Feedback Tool
Reinforces the progress of a No. 2 and provides clear, consistent expectations on their roles. (Appendix 13)

CHAPTER 10

RETAINING TOP TALENT

"People leave their bosses, not their jobs."

Most business owners believe that their employees leave them for better compensation elsewhere. I have heard owners say again and again, "If only I could have paid her more, she would have stayed." A series of studies over the past few years have proved that those sentiments are far from reality. In fact, research shows that the major reason a No. 2 stays or goes is not money. Out of all the reasons people leave jobs, there is one item that always makes the short list: a lack of leadership.

People leave their bosses, not their jobs. That's good news to business owners. It shows that retaining talent is within their control. By giving No. 2s a little more of the owner's time, personalized attention and recognition, owners can help secure their commitment to the company. That does not mean it is easy. Motivating and retaining No. 2s and other top talent in an increasingly competitive marketplace is an ongoing struggle facing organizations of all sizes.

A study completed in 2009 found that women pose twice the flight risk as men. According to Sylvia Ann Hewlett, founding president of the Center for Work-Life Policy, "We found that in the wake of (the 2009) financial crash, high-powered women were more than twice as likely as men – 84 percent compared with 40 percent – to be seriously thinking jumping ship. And when the head and heart are out the door, the rest of the body is sure to follow."

By understanding why people leave jobs, owners can create a sought-after work environment and prevent their most promising employees from walking out the door.

Here are the top reasons people leave jobs, according to talent management research:

1. Sought new challenges or opportunities (30%)
2. Ineffective leadership (25%)
3. Poor relationship with manager (22%)
4. To improve work/life balance (21%)
5. Contributions to the company were not valued (21%)
6. Better compensation and benefits (18%)

The lesson – owners have control. They can avoid making the same mistakes that led these surveyed workers to leave their jobs. They can be the boss that makes employees want to stay and maybe even tell their talented friends to apply. Owners can create an environment that fosters commitment and long-term loyalty from their No. 2s by applying these three steps into their leadership style and work routine. At the core, it's about showing No. 2s that the owner has noticed, cares and has great plans for them.

"No. 1s need to seize opportunities to understand who their No. 2s are, how they spend their time out of work and what they're most looking forward to in the next year and the next five years."

Step 1: Understand who they are

Busy owners can become disconnected when it comes to their employees. Either they are burying themselves in work, or they are too focused on the long-term vision that they fail to effectively engage in the occasional workplace small talk and truly understand what drives their employees. No. 1s can start by getting out from behind their desks and becoming a leader that walks around. Retaining a solid No. 2 requires owners to first spend some time getting to know what type of people they are. Owners do not need to get too personal, but they should learn about their No. 2s' interests, values, hobbies and home life. Likely, the No. 2s will appreciate the questions, rather than feel like owners are probing into their personal lives. It shows that the No. 1s are interested. It shows they care.

Common Traits of No. 2s

Here's what countless conversations over breakfast, lunch or company conference room tables have revealed about common No. 2 traits:

- Humility

  "Although the No. 2 is responsible for helping to carry out the strategy of the company, reach objectives and are involved in key decision making, it is the No. 1 who has the final say," said Gabe Jarnot, Northland Capital (northlandcapital.com).

- Integrity
- Prefer to not take the ultimate risk of ownership, but appreciate the responsibility and somewhat limited authority
- Take pride in handling the details without being asked.

  "It allows our No. 1 to focus his efforts in the areas in which he is truly strong and spend less time worrying about execution of the details. That has allowed us to grow through acquisition without crippling our infrastructure," Jennifer Mrozek, Marco (marconet.com).

- Not a control freak
- Extroverted
- Self-initiate
- Reach high

  "As a #2, I need to understand both sides of the fence remembering that every idea I present won't be implemented, but to continue trying to make small positive changes that will benefit everyone," said Mary Kay Pfannenstein, Mahowald Insurance (mahowald.net).

- Want all trains running on time
- Come early and stay late

Genuinely gain this information by starting Monday mornings asking them to share what they did over the weekend and their favorite part about it. Then, listen carefully and take mental notes. Starting out, No. 1s can even write it down so they remember. Owners can do the same before a weekend, holiday or the No. 2's upcoming time off. By listening for patterns and watching their body language, leaders can learn what really gets their No. 2s excited. More than anything, No. 1s need to seize opportunities to understand who their No. 2s are, how they spend their time out of work and what they're most looking forward to in the next year and the next five years.

Step 2: Understand their motivations

What keeps No. 2s at a company has been an ongoing focus of my operational and human resources work with organizations. It's a common theme during my regular meetings with No. 2s, who like to share what matters to them; and I am there to listen because it matters to the organizations for which I work. My research and insightful conversations with No. 2s show that no matter the organization or the industry, No. 2s stay for these main reasons:

Flexible work schedules

Flexible scheduling and work arrangements are becoming increasingly important to workers. Researchers from The Wake Forest University-School of Medicine find that allowing workers control over where, when and how the work is done improves commitment and reduces absenteeism. That's certainly true for No. 2s, who are willing to put in the time. They understand the company's operations, see the opportunities and appreciate the freedom to adjust their work arrangements. This may mean working from home or the ability to take off for a couple hours to attend their children's sporting events.

"Not only do No. 2s stay in their job because of it, but they also work harder for the privilege."

During my regular group breakfasts with No. 2s, they have shared that they would not be in the position if they could not work from home one day a week or have the freedom to leave for important appointments or activities. Although some owners may cringe at that flexibility and freedom, they will find it pays off in the long-term. Not only do No. 2s stay in their job because of it, but they also work harder for the privilege. Research also backs that up. A survey by the National Science Foundation found 87 percent of managers say productivity either increases or stays the same when they work from home.

Growth opportunities

No. 2s do not want the owner's job, but they do thrive on added responsibility and rewards. Following through with quarterly 15-minute feedback sessions that lead to annual performance reviews, described in Chapter 7, will help owners identify opportunities for advancement in the organization through new roles, responsibilities and key projects. At the least, No. 1s need to communicate often that they have specific plans for their No. 2. However, taking the time to articulate those plans in a more formalized professional development plan will further communicate the value of the No. 2 and solidify the No. 2's commitment to the company.

Sense of ownership

While compensation is not the main motivator of No. 2s, they are willing – and sometimes eager – to put some skin in the game through profit sharing. It is not as much about the financial payout as it is about the control, competition and job security they believe it provides. It gives them a sense of ownership, an essential element of any employee, but most definitely to a No. 2. "You can't possibly fail if your company succeeds," said Ryan Torgerson, No. 2 at Heartland Glass.

But instilling a sense of ownership in a No. 2s, as described in Chapter 8, can have nothing to do with financial incentives. Their stature in the company and responsibility to lead the team can go a long way to foster loyalty. For Lee Hurd, a longtime No. 2 at Bursch Travel, the reward comes in her ability to be a strong, sometimes courageous leader, to the travel company's management team. "Thirteen managers rely on me to hold it together," she said. "I'm in it for them." Ownership is about providing No. 2s a strong sense of value in the organization. They want to feel needed and they will prove their value when given the opportunity.

"You can't possibly fail if your company succeeds."

– Ryan Torgerson, No. 2 at Heartland Glass

Personalized rewards

While it's easy to cut a bonus check and put a little more

in the paycheck to reward a job well done, its impact fizzles far too soon. Owners that provide personalized rewards for profitable behavior see increased morale, motivation and loyalty from their No. 2s. At Heartland Glass, Ryan said the personalized gifts mean more. He still remembers the large package of minutes that owner Bill Sullivan gave him at a local golf dome. It showed Bill recognized Ryan's love for golf and encouraged him to make time to enjoy his interests outside of work.

Rewards like gift certificates to their favorite restaurant upon the completion of a project or tickets to a theater show demonstrates to No. 2s that the owners do not only recognize their job well done, but also they have taken the time to learn about their No. 2 as a person outside of the office. Perhaps this year, leaders could consider replacing the annual bonus check with a family vacation with airfare and hotel paid. It will tell their No. 2 that they value their contributions and know they value time with family.

Step 3: Know their future goals

Keeping No. 2s is not simply about fueling what drives them day to day, but also what will drive them well into the future. Owners that know their No. 2s' growth goals – personally and professionally – will be able to ensure their No. 2s see their place in the organization today and for years to come.

No. 2s do not want the owner's job, but if they feel like they hit the ceiling, they will search for a growth opportunity outside of the organization. It's important that leaders communicate how their No. 2 fits into the company's vision today and into the future. Effectively articulating that place requires owners to have some honest conversations with their No. 2s. This can occur during regular feedback sessions, over lunch or during a sit-down in the owner's office.

During these formal or informal conversations, owners should ask their No. 2s to share their professional goals for the next year, five years and 10 years. Don't be afraid to ask about their dreams and explore them. Then, use their feedback to identify opportunities and frame their future around these opportunities within the organization. Over time, owners need to revisit their No. 2's goals and dreams, see what has changed and make necessary adjustments to best align their No. 2 with the organization's vision.

Words of Appreciation

Although all of these ideas foster loyalty, owners can never underestimate the power of their words. Taking the time to say "Job Well Done!" or "I really appreciate how you really stepped up and delivered exceptional customer service under this tight deadline," mean more to employees than owners probably ever realize. They remember those words, and some, even remember the day the owners said them. Yes, that's powerful and persuasive.

It's also time well spent. Consider the cost of replacing a No. 2. It certainly varies by industry and organization, but employee turnover on average costs an estimated $15,000 for low to moderate skilled positions. Losing a No. 2 will result in more than additional costs or a financial loss; in some cases, it can cripple a company.

Are you ready?

If you can answer yes to these three questions, you're ready to move forward:

✓ Have I taken the time to learn about my No. 2's interests, values and personal motivations?

✓ Have I gained an understanding of my No. 2's future professional goals for the next year, five years and 10 years?

✓ Do I know the main reasons that keep my No. 2 with the company?

Toolbox

Use these tools to get started today. Visit *bigrivergroup.com* or flip to the Appendix for an electronic or printer-friendly versions. Gray indicates tools not yet discussed. Bold indicates tools introduced in this chapter:

Visioning Worksheet
Helps owners transfer their vision to paper and effectively communicate it. (Appendix 1)

Sample Visions
A look at how other No. 1s have put the Visioning Worksheet into practice. (Appendix 2)

Hard Skills'/Soft Skills' Worksheet
Helps owners specify what skills are needed as they search for their No. 2. (Appendix 3)

Resume Review Worksheet
Provides method to identify top candidates for No. 2 job. (Appendix 4)

Email Response Worksheet
Helps evaluate the responses to each emailed question on a three-point scale. (Appendix 5)

Interview Score Sheet
Provides scoring scale to evaluate in-depth questions based on emailed responses. (Appendix 6)

Priorities Worksheet
An owner's guide to articulating a new, perfect destination for their organizations. (Appendix 7)

Priorities to Goals Worksheet
Similar to the Priorities Worksheet, an owner's guide to translating a vision into priorities and goals. (Appendix 8)

Planning Funnel
Provides a planning process to stay on task, increase buy-in and develop a strategic plan that won't gather dust. (Appendix 9)

Outcome Diagnosis Worksheet
A planning tool that helps individuals or a team of individuals identify intended and unintended successes and challenges. (Appendix 10)

Goal Work Plan
A tool to engage a team of employees in creating a well-defined plan of action in less than 30 minutes. (Appendix 11)

My Job, Your Job
Helps translate the owners' vision into priorities and desired outcomes. (Appendix 12)

Employee Feedback Tool
Reinforces the progress of a No. 2 and provides clear, consistent expectations on their roles. (Appendix 13)

Chapter 11

Maximizing Influence

In my experience, it does not matter if you're a manual laborer or an elite-level surgeon, only about 10 percent of business leaders and owners truly understand their influence. I often find that it is because they do not recognize it and, therefore, do not take intentional steps to get results. No. 1s may be aware of influence in every other aspect of their lives – as parents, friends or even board members. But they regularly fail to maximize it in their own organization.

I know a number of employees who would "jump off a bridge" if the owner asked them to – they respect him that much. They would go to great lengths to achieve results for the owner. They want to be asked to show their loyalty. But the owner rarely recognizes it and may never capitalize on it.

Other owners that I have worked with are too focused on reaching a point so far down the road that they fail to see what's right in front of them. They miss opportunities. This is where No. 2s can help the No. 1 stop and see the opportunities to use their influence. At Heartland Glass, owner Bill Sullivan fires up the grill and cooks for his employees a couple of times a year. It may not be more than a cookout for Bill, but to his employees, it means much more. Employees shared how it made them feel valued, more connected to Bill, and wanting to work even harder because of his visible role on those days. Bill never recognized the impact of those times flipping burgers until one of his employees took the time to explain the difference it had made in that employee's performance and commitment to the company.

"Such influence takes work, some finesse and practice over time."

No. 1s often need to ask their No. 2s to coach them on practicing the art of influence. It's not a science, so there is no formula or five-step process to achieve it. Such influence takes work, some finesse and practice over time.

No. 2s can help with this process by highlighting times when the owner's influence is making a difference and identifying new opportunities.

When owners recognize their ability to use their influence, it's gold. They can make things happen quickly and foster bigger and better results. Employees respect them for it and feel valued because of it.

Take Jeff Gau, president and CEO of Marco (*marconet. com*). Since he took the helm in 2005, he has propelled the office technology firm through aggressive growth and opportunities – all for the employees' gain. The company is now 100 percent employee owned, posting strong profits despite economic challenges. Jeff has transformed what started as a small typewriter dealer in 1973 into a leading technology and office equipment company with nine offices in the Upper Midwest. The company now specializes in everything from data networking and security to print and document management to digital video conferencing and surveillance.

Spend some time with Jeff and it's clear that Jeff has a presence about him. His spirit is engaging and his leadership is inspiring. He's honest, genuine and not afraid to expose his faults. When he walks into a meeting, people notice. But it's not because he holds the title of CEO. It's because he knows how to listen, quickly build consensus and, when needed, make the hard decisions. He calls it the art of "thin-slicing." It requires him to genuinely and intently listen to each member's comments, encourage those who have not shared their thoughts to speak and communicate to everyone that he values their input. Then, he does not stutter or stall. He makes the decision. That has put Marco among the leading office technology and equipment firms in the Upper Midwest.

"Influence does not mean leaders get a line of 'yes' people."

When making a decision that affects the future of the company, Jeff shares his proposed direction and then invites all of his No. 2s to offer their perspectives, act as the devil's advocate and ask tough questions. Each No. 2 brings a different value to the table. Some are analytical and will talk about it from all angles. Some calculate risk by crunching the numbers or focusing on market share while others focus on what it will mean to the company's reputation. After hearing all sides, Jeff narrows the conversation, restates the key points and makes the decision.

Influence does not mean leaders get a line of "yes" people. For Jeff, it's quite the opposite. He depends on his No. 2s to tell him when he's out of check and challenge him so that as a team, they can make better decisions for the company.

Understanding Your Influence

Influence is not about leaders knowing – or even acting like they know – everything. Successful leaders like Jeff know their strengths and weaknesses. Jeff admits he's not a numbers guy. But he doesn't have to be, nor does he need to pretend to be. He has hired top talent to fulfill that role and he relies on the company's CFO to manage the finances. The same goes for operations and technology development. "You have to know what you're good at and be honest about what you're not, and then build your team around that," Jeff said. It comes back to a

"'You have to give up control to get control."

- Jeff Gau, President and CEO of Marco

common business line: Hire people better than you. But, Jeff said, few leaders actually do it. "You have to give up control to get control," Jeff said.

The level of influence a leader is not dictated by age or even experience. I've seen business owners in their 20s take over a room or make corporate executives bow to their expertise. I always say a good test of a leader's level of influence is if someone asks "What would (insert your name here) say?" When No. 1s use their level of influence in their organization, they make things happen by entering the room. People want them in the room because of their influence and ability to achieve results. In Chapter 10, we talked about the need for owners to recognize that their words matters. Well, an owner's actions matter also, even the small ones.

"Influential leadership also is not bound to a title."

Influential leadership also is not bound to a title. In any organization I've worked with, I can name employees who do not have impressive job titles, but still have great influence as leaders in the organization.

An Influential Leader Knows...

- Their weaknesses and hires top talent to fill them.
- How to ask the hard questions.
- When it's time to make a decision and then makes it.
- How to give up control to get control.
- How to be comfortable feeling uncomfortable.

Optimizing Your Influence

Influence can be lost when owners spend too much time off site or out of sight of employees. A leader's presence provides a visual cue that can remind employees of the vision, their role in it and the expectations. Owners that get out from behind their desk and manage by walking around post better results time and again.

When Gordy Viere started at a small CPA firm 35 years ago, he managed by walking around. He focused on sharing the company's vision and dream for the future. He wanted employees to share that dream and help him achieve it.

Today, as CEO of LarsonAllen (*larsonallen.com*), now one of the top 20 accounting firms in the world, his style hasn't changed. Gordy still knows the importance of being visible, so he makes it a point to visit every one of

LarsonAllen's locations once or twice a year. Although he cannot be at all the offices all the time, he promises to be accessible to employees by phone or email and promises to answer every email he gets from an employee. He also still participates in employee orientation, where he shares the company's vision and calls employees to be a part of what it now called the "Leader's Culture" – LarsonAllen's dream for the future.

Gordy believes that most people, if not all, want to be a part of something unique or special. They want more than a job. They desire what he calls "emotional ownership" in the company and that's what they get through the Leader's Culture.

At new hire orientation, Gordy always asks the same question: Who do you think is more important to this firm – me, the CEO with 35 years of service, or you, who has been here for one hour?" Almost every class shares the same answer: the CEO. But, that's not the answer Gordy is looking for. In a successful organization, he explains, you are the most important. You are the next leaders. It's in that moment that new hires recognize his spirit and vision of the company: For every employee to have emotional ownership. "If you can get people excited about it, they will work much harder for it," Gordy

"Gordy never attends a meeting, has a conversation or sends an email without sharing the vision. It's that important."

said. Today, Gordy never attends a meeting, has a conversation or sends an email without sharing the vision. It's that important.

Owners cannot get so wrapped up in their work that they forget to walk around, share the vision and use their influence. All too often, owners believe that by leaving their employees alone, they will allow their employees to get more work done and gain more satisfaction from their independence. That's not what employees – even No. 2s – want. They will perform better with a little contact with their leader. They want to connect with their No. 1. Give them the opportunity.

Maybe they have an idea that they want to share. Even No. 2s may not walk into the owner's office because they fear the owner is too busy or they do not want to interrupt the important work they believe their No. 1 is working on. But if leaders take a moment to walk by their No. 2's desk, magic happens – they share their idea. The owner likes it and offers some guidance on where they can take it. Then, things start happening. Progress is made – it only took a few minutes of the No. 1 stepping out of the office.

Being influential calls owners to step back, pull their head out of the future and forget about identifying future scenarios or studying external forces for a moment. Instead, successful leaders invest some time focusing on today. What's going well? What needs a little push from you? What needs your attention?

Astute No. 1s look to the future, but live in the moment. They're intentional. They're influential. But they don't go at it alone. They call on their well-groomed No. 2 to help them propel the organization to a new level – beyond any projections or predictions.

Are you ready?

This book aims to give owners and executives practical tools to find, equip and empower No. 2s to think like owners and take the organization to a new level of professionalism, purpose and profit.

No. 1s are not expected to complete every step outlined in this book, but rather work on doing parts of it really well. Review the questions below, identify two to three of them that you want to start working on next week and then share them with us at *bigrivergroup*.com so we can help you become a better leader:

Vision

✓ Have I clearly identified my vision for the organization?

✓ Do I have a clear vision with enough specifics to guide No. 2?

✓ Does my No. 2s understand my vision and can they interpret it so clearly for other employees so that those employees understand their roles and responsibilities?

✓ Does my No. 2 really understand where we're going in the next 3-5 years, and why?

Hiring a No. 2

✓ Do I really know what skill sets are needed for my No. 2?

✓ Have I determined if I can give this position to someone inside the organization?

✓ Have I designed a system that's so tight that people can't get an interview out of me without proving their worth in advance?

✓ Have I built a way for my key employees to have some input on answers to email and face-to-face interviews?

✓ Do I have enough information from semi-finalists to select a No. 2?

Continued...

Teaching

✓ Is my No. 2 asking the right kind of questions to get the job done?

✓ Do I know which leadership style (window) I use most often to teach my No.2?

✓ Do I know when to use the other styles?

✓ Have I committed 1-4-3-2 to memory as a teaching and delegation tool for my No. 2?

✓ Do I schedule quality time (not drive-by) to review and reinforce progress of my No. 2?

✓ Am I able to remove blame and emotion when talking to my No. 2s about their mistakes?

Empowering

✓ Can I identify 3-4 near-term priorities and one goal for each one?

✓ Can I identify what I want my No. 2 to accomplish for each priority? (Refer to the My Job, Your Job Worksheet from chapter 6, if necessary).

✓ Have I developed a No. 2 that thinks like an owner?

✓ Have I empowered and entrusted my No. 2 to feel like he/she can make decisions on behalf of the company?

Taking Action

Here's how owners and executives can turn this book into action steps that foster followership and help an organization thrive. Visit *bigrivergroup.com* to:

• Complete a self-assessment.

• Create an action plan to begin implementing next week.

• Sign up for tools to stay accountable and produce results.

Toolbox

Use these tools to get started today. Visit *bigrivergroup.com* or flip to the Appendix for an electronic or printer-friendly versions. Gray indicates tools not yet discussed. Bold indicates tools introduced in this chapter:

Visioning Worksheet
Helps owners transfer their vision to paper and effectively communicate it. (Appendix 1)

Sample Visions
A look at how other No. 1s have put the Visioning Worksheet into practice. (Appendix 2)

Hard Skills'/Soft Skills' Worksheet
Helps owners specify what skills are needed as they search for their No. 2. (Appendix 3)

Resume Review Worksheet
Provides method to identify top candidates for No. 2 job. (Appendix 4)

Email Response Worksheet
Helps evaluate the responses to each emailed question on a three-point scale. (Appendix 5)

Interview Score Sheet
Provides scoring scale to evaluate in-depth questions based on emailed responses. (Appendix 6)

Priorities Worksheet
An owner's guide to articulating a new, perfect destination for their organizations. (Appendix 7)

Priorities to Goals Worksheet
Similar to the Priorities Worksheet, an owner's guide to translating a vision into priorities and goals. (Appendix 8)

Planning Funnel
Provides a planning process to stay on task, increase buy-in and develop a strategic plan that won't gather dust. (Appendix 9)

Outcome Diagnosis Worksheet
A planning tool that helps individuals or a team of individuals identify intended and unintended successes and challenges. (Appendix 10)

Goal Work Plan
A tool to engage a team of employees in creating a well-defined plan of action in less than 30 minutes. (Appendix 11)

My Job, Your Job
Helps translate the owners' vision into priorities and desired outcomes. (Appendix 12)

Employee Feedback Tool
Reinforces the progress of a No. 2 and provides clear, consistent expectations on their roles. (Appendix 13)

Appendix

Visioning Worksheet

Helps owners transfer their vision to paper and effectively communicate it. (Appendix 1)

Sample Visions

A look at how other No. 1s have put the Visioning Worksheet into practice. (Appendix 2)

Hard Skills/Soft Skills Worksheet

Helps owners specify what skills are needed as they search for their No. 2. (Appendix 3)

Resume Review Worksheet

Provides method to identify top candidates for No. 2 job. (Appendix 4)

Email Response Worksheet

Helps evaluate the responses to each emailed question on a three-point scale. (Appendix 5)

Interview Score Sheet

Provides scoring scale to evaluate in-depth questions based on emailed responses. (Appendix 6)

Priorities Worksheet

An owner's guide to articulating a new, perfect destination for their organizations. (Appendix 7)

Priorities to Goals Worksheet

Similar to the Priorities Worksheet, an owner's guide to translating a vision into priorities and goals. (Appendix 8)

Planning Funnel

Provides a planning process to stay on task, increase buy-in and develop a strategic plan that won't gather dust. (Appendix 9)

Outcome Diagnosis Worksheet

A planning tool that helps individuals or a team of individuals identify intended and unintended successes and challenges. (Appendix 10)

Goal Work Plan

A tool to engage a team of employees in creating a well-defined plan of action in less than 30 minutes. (Appendix 11)

My Job, Your Job

Helps translate the owners' vision into priorities and desired outcomes. (Appendix 12)

Employee Feedback Tool

Reinforces the progress of a No. 2 and provides clear, consistent expectations on their roles. (Appendix 13)

VISIONING WORKSHEET

BIG RIVER
Consulting Group, LLC
P.O. Box 5120 · St. Cloud, MN 56302-5120
(800) 500-7017 · Fax (320) 202-1010
Bruce@bigrivergroup.com

Chainsaw Planning©

Owner's Vision Worksheet

1) What will your business look like 3 to 5 years from now?

2) Describe your ideal sales mix: products & services.

3) What will your client portfolio/mix look like?

4) Describe in detail your operations & financial procedures.

5) How will your key employees spend their time?

6) What will your sales sequence look like?

7) How will you sophisticate & differentiate your marketing?

8) What will your customer experience look like?

9) How will you spend your time?

2010 © Big River Group, LLC

SAMPLE VISIONS

Sample Vision & Mission Statements

Vision Statements Describe *New Destinations.*

- An ideal organization
  "We will become a top-ten University"
  "The best restaurant in town: Your first choice for fine dining"

- Ideal services
  "The Auto Glass Company that provides the best customer service"
  "The Restaurant that provides unmatched attention & service"

- Ideal lives
  "Developing a cure for cancer before 2010"

- Ideal products
  "Producing flawless vehicles at a reasonable cost"
  "A 200-pound buck hanging in a tree by 10:00 AM Saturday"

Mission Statements are *Job Descriptions.*

- What an organization will do
  "Provide an excellent university education at an average price"
  "Provide the best food and the best service in our area"

- What services will be provided
  "We make our customers' lives easier by replacing all auto glass
       with no disruption in their work or home schedules"
  "Need credit? Bad credit? We arrange loans for anyone"

- How lives will be changed
  "Providing an exceptional environment & instruction, & first-
  class equipment to help our customers improve fitness"

- What products will be delivered
  "On-time delivery, every time"
  "A deer hunt with flawless planning & attention to detail"

2010 © Big River Group, LLC

BIG RIVER
Consulting Group, LLC
P.O. Box 5120 · St. Cloud, MN 56302-5120
(800) 500-7017 · Fax (320) 202-1010
Bruce@bigrivergroup.com

HARD SKILLS/SOFT SKILLS WORKSHEET

No. 2 POSITION TITLE: _____

DESIRED HARD SKILLS	DESIRED SOFT SKILLS
1.	1.
2.	2.
3.	3.
4.	4.
5.	5.

2010 © Big River Group, LLC

RESUME REVIEW WORKSHEET

Date: _____

Organization: _____

Position to be Hired: _____ **Applicant:** _____

Vision, Mission or Core Beliefs: _____

Priorities or Goals for This Position:

1)

2)

3)

	1) Score: +, 0, - Goal #1	*2)* Score: +, 0, - Goal #2	*3)* Score: +, 0, - Goal #3
1) Sorter #1 Name:			
2) Sorter #2 Name:			
3) Sorter #3 Name:			
4) Sorter #4 Name:			
5) Sorter #5 Name:			

6) Extra Credit?

2010 © Big River Group, LLC

EMAIL RESPONSE WORKSHEET

Big River Consulting Group, LLC
P.O. Box 5120 · St. Cloud, MN 56302-5120
(800) 500-7017 · Fax (320) 202-1010
Bruce@bigrivergroup.com

Date: _____

Organization: _____

Position to be Hired: _____ **Applicant:** _____

Vision, Mission or Core Beliefs: _____

Priorities or Goals for This Position:

    1)

    2)

    3)

----

	1) Score: +, 0, - Goal #1	2) Score: +, 0, - Goal #2	3) Score: +, 0, - Goal #3
1) Sorter #1 Name:			
2) Sorter #2 Name:			
3) Sorter #3 Name:			
4) Sorter #4 Name:			
5) Sorter #5 Name:			

6) Extra Credit?

2010 © Big River Group, LLC

INTERVIEW SCORE SHEET

Date: _____

Department: _____

Position to be Hired: _____   Applicant: _____

Interviewers: _____

Priorities or Goals for This Position:

    1)

    2)

    3)

                                   Score (+, 0, -) & Notes   Extra Credit: Reason?

1) Question #1
   Topic:
----

2) Question #2
   Topic:
----

3) Question #3
   Topic:
----

4) Question #4
   Topic:
----

5) Question #5
   Topic: Best Idea Ever
----

6) Other Items?

2010 © Big River Group, LLC

PRIORITIES WORKSHEET

Write your organization's new _Vision_ here.

Write your organization's new _Mission_ here.

Identify between 4 - 6 _Priorities_.

1)

2)

3)

4)

5)
(optional)

6)
(optional)

2010 © Big River Group, LLC

PRIORITIES TO GOALS WORKSHEET

Priority #1
> **Goal**
> **Goal**
> **Goal**

Priority #2
> **Goal**
> **Goal**
> **Goal**

Priority #3
> **Goal**
> **Goal**
> **Goal**

Priority #4
> **Goal**
> **Goal**
> **Goal**

Priority #5
> **Goal**
> **Goal**
> **Goal**

Priority #6
> **Goal**
> **Goal**
> **Goal**

2010 © Big River Group, LLC

PLANNING FUNNEL

BIG RIVER
Consulting Group, LLC
P.O. Box 5120 · St. Cloud, MN 56302-5120
(800) 500-7017 · Fax (320) 202-1010
Bruce@bigrivergroup.com

Data
(Hard data & soft data)

Vision
(A new, perfect destination)

Mission
(Job description to get there)

Priorities
(Essential Items)

Specific Goals

*Detailed
Work
Plans*

2010 © Big River Group, LLC

OUTCOME DIAGNOSIS WORKSHEET

	Positive	Less Than Positive
Intended	1. 2. 3. 4. 5.	1. 2. 3. 4. 5.
Unintended	1. 2. 3. 4. 5.	1. 2. 3. 4. 5.

2010 © Big River Group, LLC

GOAL WORK PLAN

BIG RIVER
Consulting Group, LLC
P.O. Box 5120 · St. Cloud, MN 56302-5120
(800) 500-7017 · Fax (320) 202-1010
Bruce@bigrivergroup.com

Admiration of the Problem (ID all sub-issues & hurdles; 5 minutes)

SMART Goal (specific, measurable, attainable, realistic and timely)
(in 20 words or less; 5 minutes)

Objectives / Action Steps (≤4; 10 minutes)

1)

2)

3)

4)

Timeline (desired per objective)	**Resources** (needed per objective)	**Responsibility** (name per objective)
1)	1)	1)
2)	2)	2)
3)	3)	3)
4)	4)	4)

Evaluation Plan (Quantitative and/or Qualitative; 5 minutes)

Quantitative:

Qualitative:

2010 © Big River Group, LLC

MY JOB, YOUR JOB

BIG RIVER
Consulting Group, LLC
P.O. Box 5120 · St. Cloud, MN 56302-5120
(800) 500-7017 · Fax (320) 202-1010
Bruce@bigrivergroup.com

Worksheet: My Job, Your Job
(Organization)
(Today's Date)
(Desired Time Period)

Organizational Leaders

1)   2)   3)   4)   5)

Priority 1:

Goal 1:

Priority 2:

Goal 2:

Priority 3:

Goal 3:

Priority 4:

Goal 4:

Priority 5:

Goal 5:

Priority 6:

Goal 6:

Project Notes:

1)
2)
3)
4)
5)

2010 © Big River Group, LLC

EMPLOYEE FEEDBACK TOOL

Big River Consulting Group, LLC

P.O. Box 5120 · St. Cloud, MN 56302-5120
(800) 500-7017 · Fax (320) 202-1010
Bruce@bigrivergroup.com

Employee: _____
Manager: _____
Date: _____

Employee Feedback Form

Other Performance

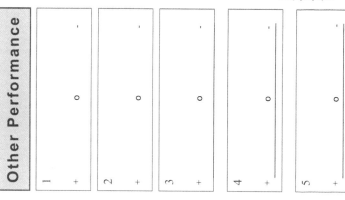

1 + − o
2 + − o
3 + − o
4 + − o
5 + − o

Personal Goals

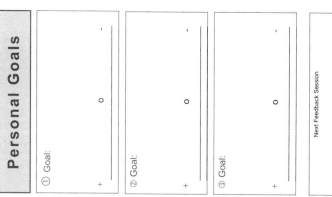

① Goal: + − o

② Goal: + − o

③ Goal: + − o

Next Feedback Session

_____ (Day) _____ (Month) _____ (Year)

Company Goals

Priority #1
Goal:

Priority #2
Goal:

Priority #3
Goal:

Priority #4
Goal:

Priority #5
Goal:

2010 © Big River Group, LLC